WITHDRAWN

The Human Side of
STATISTICAL
CONSULTING

JAMES R. BOEN

DOUGLAS A. ZAHN

Lifetime Learning Publications
A division of Wadsworth, Inc.
Belmont, California

London, Singapore, Sydney
Toronto, Mexico City

Designer: Nancy Benedict
Copy Editor: Sylvia Stein

Printed in the United States of America
1 2 3 4 5 6 7 8 9 10—86 85 84 83 82

Library of Congress Cataloging in Publication Data
Boen, James R., 1932–
   The human side of statistical consulting.

   Bibliography: p.
   Includes index.
   1. Statistical consultants. I. Zahn, Douglas A.,
1943–   . II. Title.
QA276.17.B63   001.4'22'023   81–17232
ISBN 0-534-97949-1   AACR2

Contents

ACKNOWLEDGMENTS

The authors are indebted to many colleagues for helpful conversations. The authors are also grateful to Kay Dressler, Karen Cox, and Susan Lincicome for their patience and skill in typing the manuscript.

Preface

This book is the authors' response to the lack of realistic consulting experiences available to statistics students and those new to the field. It is well known, perfectly understandable, and widely accepted that colleges and universities do not fully prepare their graduates for "success on the job" as judged by nonacademic employers. Our aim is to contribute to closing the gap between academic training and on-the-job requirements by providing an extensive discussion of our experiences as statistical consultants and some general principles of effective statistical consulting.

The essence of statistical consulting is the embedding of high technical skill in the real world of time, money, and office politics. As such, it is a highly complex endeavor.

Statistics graduates emerge from school with technical strength, but unaware of the demands of industry and government. Graduates are apprehensive enough about their technical ability, let alone corporate realities. They soon learn that statistical consultation has statistical and nonstatistical components. Skills in both areas are essential if they are to be effective consultants. One focus of this book is to help the apprentice statistical consultant develop nonstatistical skills and make the school-to-work adjustment.

This book is intended to shorten the time of transition from pink cheeks to seasoned veteran. It will be of use both to graduate students in supervised consulting courses and to apprentice statistical consultants, new on the job. We also intend to reduce the pain of the adjustment. To this latter end, we tell a few tales on ourselves. We didn't win them all, but we sure didn't lose them all either. We think these cases will prove to be thought provoking, even for seasoned consultants. We even hope that seasoned veterans see some new slants on their interactions with their clients by reading our perceptions of our interactions with our clients. What works for you in similar situations? We look forward to hearing from you.

If you have to have formulas and data in your applied statistics books, read no further. There aren't any in this book. We bow to other authors in these areas and generally use only English words. We hope you read it, enjoy it, and, because we keep learning ourselves, tell us what you think.

Jim Boen and Doug Zahn

CHAPTER 1

What Is Statistical Consultation?

There is so much consultation going on in so many contexts that everybody has an image of what consultation is and what consultants are like. Images range from that of an intelligent, informed adviser who offers helpful suggestions without interfering to that of a fast talker who enters with colored slides, only to carry away high fees. The word *consultation* conjures up for many statisticians an image of a shallow relationship in which the consultant learns too little of the scientific problem. Many statisticians thus reserve the word *collaboration* for the ideal, deep, equal-status relationship between statistician and scientist.

In this book, we're going to use the word *consultation* to cover a wide variety of relationships, from the quick visit lasting ten minutes to collaborative ones lasting several years.

What the relationships have in common is that the main goal of the interaction is to help the field of application, not the field of statistics.

There is one kind of interaction between statisticians and scientists that we do *not* call consultation. It differs from what we call consultation in that the statistician's primary purpose is not to assist the scientist, but to be stimulated to new research in statistics. This motive to interact with scientists for statistical stimulation is the natural motive of professors who want to publish in statistics journals. Occasionally, this motivation results in a satisfied client and good science. Our main reason for excluding statistician-scientist interaction in which the former's primary intent is stimulation for statistical research is that what we have to say in this book will be of little interest to such a statistician. This book is intended primarily for the beginning consultant whose salary and job security depend on having satisfied clients.

CLIENT SATISFACTION

Clients experience satisfaction when they and the statistical consultant work together and get the job done. Getting the job done means that consultant and client understand the limits and extent of the data they have and the statistical tools they used. They have used the tools appropriately and communicated the results effectively to others. Getting the job done does *not* mean making a silk purse out of a sow's ear, but telling the truth about what is in the data. If a design error results in no inferences being possible, then the effective consultant and the client clearly report to their audiences that no inferences were possible because of the design error. The saisfied client is not necessarily comfortable. Comfort is not the same as satisfaction. Comfort at the cost of not getting the job done does not last and is not satisfying.

Turner (1979) describes two models for the consulting process. In his first, he emphasizes the consultant's problem-solving ability. The client is asking the consultant for a solution to a problem. The consultant may take the problem and go away and work on it. The main outcome will be a written and/or verbal presentation by the consultant to the client of the analyses and the findings. The second model emphasizes client achievement and learning. The client is looking for ways to improve his or her research methodology and statistical operations. The emphasis is on the consultant working with the client to clarify goals and develop proposals that are consistent with the client's situation and that will achieve the latter's goals. Both models are correct. The choice depends on the consultant, the client, and the problem.

CONSULTANT RESPONSIBILITY

Is it the statistician's responsibility to choose only theoretically optimal procedures? Shall he or she not be satisfied until the "best" analysis has been done? Few authors in the statistical literature have attempted to make a comprehensive list of the statistical consultant's responsibilities. Marquardt (1979) lists in Table 1 the statistical consultant's responsibilities if he or she is practicing what Marquardt calls "total involvement consulting." The responsibility in this list that catches our eyes is "devise a statistically sound plan of action." Note that this responsibility emphasizes a *sound* course of action rather than the mathematically *optimal* technique. This highlights the distinction between what professors expect of you and what industry or government expects of you. Outside the classroom, the emphasis is on compromise forced by real-world constraints.

Fitting statistical theory to practice is enormously challenging and an opportunity to be creative. It requires intellect, imagination, and creativity as much as any academic pursuit and is done subject to the real-world constraints of time, money, and politics.

CHAPTER 2

The Work of Consulting

For the reader who is deciding whether to take a job in statistical consulting, we offer our views of its noneconomic rewards. Some of our wisdom is based on our own experiences; even though we are professors, we have heavy loads of consulting, with time and money pressures. Most of our clients are within our universities, but a few are from industry and government. Our other main experience is in educating statistics students for consulting (teaching and grading consulting courses) and helping them decide whether the consulting life is right for them. There are several different kinds of rewards for the statistical consultant, beyond the obvious monetary ones. One is the satisfaction of solving a statistics problem that isn't in a textbook with the answer in the back. The clients won't know whether you're correct. However, common sense will help guide them. You might never even know if you are correct.

LACK OF ROLE MODELS

Statistics is a low-profile field, and the public doesn't see conspicious role models of statistical consultants. There are doctors and lawyers everywhere, including on TV; so people who want to know what it's like to practice medicine or law have plenty of chances to observe. It is uncommon for statistics professors to be accurate describers of the consulting life. Many professors simply don't do it or do it in the purest academic setting without money or time constraints. Furthermore, their clients are their collaborators and co-authors of academic papers and don't present serious relationship difficulties.

However, there are role models available to some statistics graduate students. If the student is in a department with a consulting center, its staff offers examples of statistical consultants in an academic setting. Similarly, if new graduates join the consulting group in a large company at the beginning of their career, there will be role models in that group.

VARIETY OF CLIENTS

One's perception of what it is like to consult depends on the situation and the consultant's personality. There is a wide variety of types of clientele from many substantive areas; so all statisticians like working with some of them. Clients come with greatly varying degrees of intelligence, dedication to their work, honesty, and pleasantness of personality. Some are fiercely proud and resent the statistical ignorance that requires them to need help. At the other extreme are clients who like being dependent on statistical experts, even to the point of getting statisticians to make decisions outside their area. There are clients who are consumed with their own research and who identify very personally with success and failure in their work. Others act indifferent to their research, exhibiting a take-it-or-leave-it attitude, and are sometimes even careless. There are clients who exude integrity and clients who seem covert.

Many statisticians like the variety of consulting with clients from different fields who are glad to teach a bit of their substantive specialty to a helpful consultant. We find it very stimulating to interact with heterogeneous groups of clients. Many of them are at the cutting edge of their disciplines, pushing out the frontiers in their areas of research and encountering new statistical problems. These people are alive with enthusiasm and energy and easily infect us with their spirit. From working with them, we gain a sense of having helped to understand the world.

A NEW CHALLENGE

One of the challenges encountered by the beginning consultant is the adjustment from school to work. Formal statistics education is full of so many theories and concepts that little time is left to prepare for the realities of being a statistician in government or industry. The main shock is the chaos of a consulting statistician's life, the challenge of doing statistics and science in an atmosphere of time, money, and office politics. This shock occurs regardless of whether students go into government, industry, academia, or a consulting firm.

Young consultants may have to make hard decisions and compromises without a kindly, parental, teacher figure holding their hand and assuring them they are doing the right thing. However, if they have joined a statistical consulting group, there will be mentors around to aid in the school-to-job transition. Consulting is much less structured than school statistics courses.

THE REWARDS

Growth and Development

The history of statistics is full of stories of the great statisticians who rose to eminence from mundane jobs. They found inspiration in their work and made brilliant generalizations. Growth and development as a statistician are possible rewards of a career as a statistical consultant.

Contributions to Science

Still another reward is the feeling of making the world a better place by helping science proceed more efficiently and with fewer false leads caused by inappropriate designs and data analyses.

Satisfying Relationships

There is an additional, distinctly different reward category not typically mentioned in the literature on statistical consultation. It is the satisfaction in relationships you form with your clients. The kinds of relationships that statisticians form with their clients vary with all the kinds of consultants and clients there are. These relationships can stretch over many years. There are statisticians who enjoy most of their clients immensely.

Challenging Problems

One of the most rewarding experiences for us in statistical consulting occurs when we unscramble a very difficult consulting problem. The experience is more exciting if the job also has to be done under tight time constraints. The whole interaction then leaves us feeling exhilarated and exhausted. During such cases, we often feel tense, nervous, and excited by the "thrill of the chase." The exhilaration makes up for the tenseness. For example, one Monday morning at eleven o'clock, a researcher entered my office with data showing schoolchildren's deaths due to daylight savings time.* He asked me to analyze these data because the state legislature was going to meet at nine the next morning to begin considering whether daylight savings time should be repealed. I dropped everything else and threw all of my resources (including some willing colleagues) into the problem. We called around the country to find who might have information on this case. We also contacted the national weather center for information on how foggy it had been in Florida during that January. Then the data, which consisted of several two-by-two contingency tables, were analyzed and reanalyzed into the wee hours of the morning. We wrote the report and had it typed in time for the legislature committee meeting. The difference in death rates between the daylight savings time of that year and previous standard time years was "small." The report took that emotion out of the issue, and the legislature went on to focus on the political and economic aspects.

Statistical consulting also allows us to play detective. On some cases, we have fantasies of being Sherlock Holmes, gathering information from many sources to support the statistical work. A case that comes to mind involved the analysis of a large data set. Through following up leads, hunches, and pieces of intuition, I asked a series of questions that led to the discovery of a substantial portion of the data set prepared by the previous team that had been erroneously placed in computer storage. Although I was chagrined to find out this error had been made, I was proud to discover it before additional effort had been wasted.

Client's Gratitude

One of the greatest rewards is the gratitude of a client who feels rescued and remains grateful. We have become heroes in the eyes of some clients and cherish the warm

---

*All the anecdotes about clients and personal revelations of the authors are real. To offer maximum protection for both authors and clients through anonymity, we made three alterations to reality: (1) almost all clients' names are fictitious; (2) some gender identifications are fictitious; and (3) we do not identify ourselves (except for one instance) in our use of "I" in personal revelations or anecdotes about clients.

glow. Occasionally, there are some we want to avoid. Here are some examples of our feelings toward our clients.

Dr. Y.   I didn't know who Dr. Y was when she called me one morning. I was only moderately busy with some light administrative paperwork and thus able to concentrate on her request. She was in a rush to see me because of an immediate research contract application deadline. Dr. Y started to explain the details of the contract, that it was research on deficiency, but I said I couldn't absorb much detail over the phone. We made an appointment for early the next morning.

Dr. Y gave every impression of vigor, intelligence, and high ego strength. She was about thirty, tall, and looked strong and healthy. Although with much minority blood (I'm not sure whether it is Asian or Native American), Dr. Y was totally Americanized. She expressed herself clearly and directly and listened attentively to me. She got to the point, that the contract she was applying for with a senior investigator had mixed blessings and called for a somewhat unrealistic design. Still, she and her senior partner wanted to go for it because they had a "30 percent chance" of getting it. There were some parts of the contract that were possible and worthwhile, and they would just have to put up with the bad parts. They would have had a much better chance if a certain researcher at another university would join them in the application, but Dr. Y said that potential collaborator was being courted to collaborate with another applicant team.

We talked about the pros and cons of the design, partly a randomized clinical trial. It called for way too much matching, however, so much so that no investigator could strictly carry out the contract. We wondered how serious and how smart was the group who made it up.

The senior investigator, Dr. P, had sent Dr. Y to see me; Dr. Y's assignment was to get me to join them as a consultant to the project. I was also to arrange for keypunching, coding, and programming and estimate the cost. I was worried about signing up to work with Dr. P because I knew he tends to measure too many variables on too few subjects and create big multiple inference problems. He also gets too excited about statistical significance. No one can talk him out of publishing correlations with p-values of .04 on relationships that make no a priori scientific sense and that are chosen from a long list of correlations. Dr. P is a generally conscientious person, however, and a very unselfish clinician who does his research in areas where it is ethically impossible to perform randomized clinical trials. I decided to say yes, encouraged by the fact that Dr. Y would be working on the project and would probably help me in my battles with Dr. P. They were ordered by the contract people to have a statistician help them.

One moral of this story is that it is all right to not handle every request for statistical consultation on the phone in the same phone call that originated the request. It is usually impossible. A similar response is effective for clients who have "one quick question that will take just a minute of your time," if you can only drop what you are doing to pay attention to them. To such clients, we say, "In my experience, no statistical answer takes just a minute. Can we spend five minutes on it? If five minutes isn't enough, I would be willing to schedule a regular appointment. Now, I'd like to hear your question."

Dr. V. Although Jack's ten years older than I am, we have a good time talking about our kids and buying houses. We also used to exchange jokes; we urged each other to come up with some good ones. Jack's a great laugher.

Jack has a Ph.D. in a basic science and is very hard working. His political views put him in disfavor with his department chairman, but he doesn't butter up anyone. He is very scrupulous and intense in his work. We collaborated on a couple of papers, and he was terrific to work with. He gave me total statistical authority and incorporated most of my design suggestions. It was very satisfying. Sadly, the research grants in Jack's area dried up and I now just bump into him occasionally. He's mainly teaching and doing heavy committee work. For several years he was my favorite client. We have great mutual trust and respect.

Dr. H.   I have known Dr. H for fifteen years. We occasionally run into each other at musical events, but he stopped being my client several years ago. He's nice as can be to me, as he is to everyone else, but I probably alienated him with the hard-nose approach I used on him the last time. I became frustrated with Dr. H when he sent a junior colleague to see me with an impossible request. The colleague probably went back to Dr. H and told him I was too rigid to work with. Dr. H has used several of my colleagues as statistical consultants and clearly prefers a statistician with a gentle personality.

Dr. H is extremely conscientious and well intentioned but many people have a hard time working with him. Perhaps he so hates to bother his consultants that as soon as they start to give him some advice, he says he understands it and will take it from there. He then drops out of sight for two months. When he comes back, however, it seems as though he forgot what the consultant said, and he asks the same questions again. No one is sure why he does this. It could be that he is bluffing and wants to appear bright, but that is not likely the case. He may be so hesitant to impose that when his consultants start to clarify, he thinks he's being a nuisance.

A colleague found something very exciting in Dr. H's data that contradicted widely accepted theories. Dr. H was visibly upset at the thought of his entering into controversy and thus inevitably hurting someone's feelings. He's so humble that all who consult with him are tempted to reassure and comfort him. But he's a great clinician. I sent my own mother to him when she had a problem in his area of expertise.

Dr. F.   I just can't stand Dr. F. I'll admit to being a tiny bit manipulative, but Dr. F's style of manipulation nauseates me. She tries to get statisticians into the most complicated coworker relationships. If one falls into her clutches, there are likely to be calls at any time of the week or weekend, day or night. Dr. F pours a ton of honey on the statistician and expects total personal loyalty from then on. She's done this number on every statistician on this campus and who knows how many other campuses. Each time she runs out of the rest of them and is forced to come back to me, I'm more angry than the time before. I just want her to go away and never bother me again.

A Good Future

A comforting feature of statistical consulting comes from the fact that client demand for good consultants is high and on the increase. We are apparently in a growth profession. There will probably be ample opportunities for effective statistical consultants to enjoy their job, make a nice living, and do the world some good.

SUMMARY

• Consulting can develop you as a statistician. It offers you an opportunity to grow and is very challenging.

• You can find social satisfaction in consulting and form lasting friendships.

• Good consulting helps improve the world.

• Consulting can be exciting, especially when you pull together information from diverse sources to solve a thorny problem.

• You can learn about new developments in many fields from your clients.

CHAPTER 3

Client and Peer Expectations

How much should you know? You can never know too much. And the more you know, the better. If someone asks, "I want to become a better consultant. I have time and energy to spend doing so and would not take it out of time and energy spent on learning science or computing. It would come out of my recreation time. Should I get more book knowledge of statistics?", the answer is a resounding yes. And it doesn't matter how much the questioner already knows. Nobody knows too much. The more statistics you know, the better.

LICENSURE AND MINIMUM STANDARDS

The question of how much statistics you have to know to be a consultant gets interesting when we seriously discuss minimum knowledge. Is there an *official* minimum knowledge? No. The only existing organization that might have the authority to decide on minimum knowledge is the American Statistical Association (ASA), but it hasn't done so.

Certification

The topic of certification of statisticians has come up in the ASA from time to time, but it never gets off the ground. Certification means that the ASA would publish a list of statisticians of whom it approves as practitioners. Potential clients could use the list as a shopping guide to find a consultant or to see whether the person selected as a consultant is ASA approved. A brief paper by Boen and Smith (1975) aroused no discernible interest in the topic. As it stands, there is neither an official minimum knowledge of statistics nor an official list of approved schools from which one must have graduated. (The criterion of graduation from an approved school is called *accreditation*.) Statistics is a long way from permissive licensure and even further from mandatory licensure. Medicine, for example, has mandatory licensure. This means you are fined or jailed for taking money for doing what doctors do. In other words, you can't take money for doing surgery on someone, even if you don't call yourself a doctor. Permissive licensure means you can't take money for giving people talk therapy while calling yourself a registered psychologist. But with *permissive licensure,* you can take money for giving talk therapy if you just don't *call* yourself a registered psychologist. These legal protections of job territories are state laws.

Because there is no official minimum knowledge for a statistical consultant, persons with one statistics course under their belt can hang out a shingle and call themselves statisticians. To consummate that status, they need only one client who thinks of them as a consultant. Although most of this book is accessible to the one-statistics-course consultant, we do have our own working definition of minimum knowledge. We do it knowing full well how arbitrary and imperfect it is. We think the minimum academic knowledge to be a statistical consultant is the *equivalent* of a master's degree in statistics. We arrived at this view after years of teaching graduate students in biometry and statistics and seeing at what level we feel comfortable letting them have their own clients. Of course, there are exceptional people with only a bachelor's degree in statistics or a master's degree in operations research who have great statistical talent. There are even outstanding statisticians who have no degree in statistics but have learned it on their own.

Competencies

A list of statistical techniques used by industry was offered by Snee et al. (1980). They are listed in groups in order of decreasing frequency of use. The first five competencies are essential. Beyond the first five, the order of importance depends on the clientele and the practice. Survey sampling, for example, is much more important to the survey statistician than is bioassay.

Regression analysis
Basic statistical methods
Analysis of variance
Graphical display and data summary
Design of experiments

Variance-component estimation
Biostatistics, including bioassay
Categorical data analysis
Quality control and acceptance sampling
Nonlinear estimation
Nonparametric methods
Ranking/paired comparison data analysis
Multivariate analysis

Probability modeling
Simulation

Reliability and life data analysis
Numerical analysis
Time series analysis
Survey sampling

A word of caution: You can still be a very good statistical consultant without knowing all these well. Anybody who knows all these well has ideal knowledge. Those completely ignorant of one or more of the first five should limit themselves to restricted consultation and caution any client about thinking of them as a knowledgeable general purpose consultant.

Lack of Official Criteria

The ASA has not set official minimum criteria and we do not expect it to do so in the near future. The people who are, in effect, answering the question are clients. If you're reading this book, you probably already know that many clients are poor judges of how much statistics their consultant ought to know. It is very common for a client who is, say, a microbiologist to seek statistical advice from another microbiologist who's had a couple of statistics courses rather than seek out a statistician. The clients do that for several reasons. For one, they may think there is so little to know about statistics that someone who has taken a couple of courses knows it all. Another reason is that full-fledged statisticians are hard to find, even with an ASA directory. A third is that the word is out: Full-fledged statisticians can be difficult to work with.

STATISTICIANS' ATTITUDES

Being a good statistical consultant means knowing more than statistics. There are nonstatistical components in effective statistical consultation. Take the guy who is an absolute whiz at mathematical statistics but knows very little science and is condescending toward scientists. Will he be more help to the microbiologist than a microbiologist who's had a couple of statistics courses? Not likely. The statistician should know something about microbiology if he's going to be of help, and that takes some time. Another reason he's not necessarily better is his attitude. The microbiologist client may be so upset by the statistician's attitude that the client just won't work with him.

The attitudinal difference between the statistician and the microbiologist "statistical consultant" illustrates one of the most important aspects of the nonstatistical side of statistical consulting. The microbiologist "statistical consultant" is more likely to think the microbiologist client can learn the statistical concepts because she herself did. Thinking that the client is capable of the statistical concepts has a profound effect on your strategy. Some statistical consultants believe clients cannot understand concepts of statistics. Whether the client understands is a question of your and the client's intent and the time investment that the two of you are willing to make. The question here is whose responsibility it is that the client learn.

We now approach clients assuming that they are capable of comprehending the statistical explanation and that both of us are responsible for getting the explanation across. We feel rewarded by the results. Perseverance has led to successful communications with clients we would have given up on three years ago.

YOUR CLIENT'S NEEDS

Of course, not all clients want the same thing. Being technical about it, no two clients want *exactly* the same thing. However, there are some general principles. Patients seek help from doctors; students seek help from teachers; and scientists and others seek help from statisticians. The patient, student, or client have something in common: they are *dependent* on these experts, and that can intimidate them. There are many other helper-helpee relationships, but we draw analogies from doctor-patient and teacher-student relationships because each of you has probably been both a patient and a student.

Know Your Stuff

First and foremost, you want your doctor to know medicine and your teacher to know the subject. Your clients want you to know statistics. There is no point in clients coming to see you if you aren't an expert, at least relative to them. This obviously does not mean that you must memorize the entire statistical literature. You should know how to do a t-test or a Wilcoxon two-sample test and the relative advantages of the two procedures, but it is appropriate to look up the formulas for multiple comparisons procedures. To make themselves feel better, clients may even psych themselves into believing you are more knowledgeable than any statistician really is. Once a helpee has chosen a helper, the helpee wants to believe the choice was good. We'll discuss later what to do about expectations of your client and yourself relative to knowledge. These expectations are an enormous burden for statisticians.

Arrange for Allied Services

When your doctor says you need a chest X-ray, you don't want to start thumbing through the yellow pages to find an X-ray technician. You don't expect your doctor to take the X-ray, but the receptionist should be able to tell you when and where to get it taken. You expect the X-ray technician to know who your doctor is, to know that he's legitimate, and to respect his judgment. You expect the X-ray to be read by someone who knows what she's doing (if your doctor doesn't read it) and get the report back to him quickly. In other words, you want your doctor to arrange for all the aspects of diagnosis and treatment of your illness. You want him to have many contacts with good, appropriate people and put you into systems that *work*. If he doesn't, you hold him responsible.

Similarly, your client may want you to have contacts and good arrangements with the allied services of statistics. Such clients want to give you the problem and have you arrange for coding, keying, programming, graphing, and typing of reports. They want to have just one contact—you—arrange for and be responsible for everything associated with the statistics.

One of us provides for allied services, but the other does not. In the latter case, clients are responsible for arranging their statistical services, such as keypunching, programming, and computer work; the consultant provides only the non-standard statistical aspects of the work. Though our two consulting operations are both in a university setting, our modes of operation are considerably different. The intent in both centers is the same, namely, providing statistical consulting to the clients.

Manage Time and Money

You want your doctor to estimate how long your treatment will take and how much it will cost. Your client wants the same from you. Money might or might not be an issue. It may not be if you work for the same company and are both on salaries, but the issue of cross-charge from your department to your client's could arise and he or she will want to know how much it will cost, including your time, coding, keying, and programming.

Time is always a factor. Clients want to know when it will be done. The more you tell them what will happen when, the better they will like it. They want you to be good at business and at managing time and money.

Loyalty

Your clients want you to help them, not do things to hurt them. They do not want to be ridiculed when you talk about them to other people. They want you to be on their side, emphasizing the good aspects of them and their work, and deemphasizing the bad aspects.

Compassion

You want your doctor to forgive you for not getting all the checkups you should, for not taking off weight, for smoking too much. You want teachers to forgive you for being bored with their subjects, for not keeping up with your homework. You want your doctor to set aside his anger at your not taking better care of yourself and still do his best to treat you. You want your teacher to forgive you for being poorly prepared and still deliver all her lectures with clarity, wit, and enthusiasm.

Your clients want you to forgive them for the many things they know they have done wrong. They want you to overlook the fact that they haven't seen you before beginning the study and that they are not as good at math and statistics as they want to be. They want you to be tolerant and not be curt with them for not understanding your explanations. They want you not to be angry when they ask you to suggest a sample size even though they can't decide on what a meaningful alternative hypothesis is or what power they want. They want you to contain your frustration when their problem is hopelessly messy or when there are heavy political pressures on them that compromise their science. They want to be forgiven for not planning their time well and asking you to accommodate your schedule to theirs. They want you, in spite of all their shortcomings and inconsideration, to be of constant good cheer and do your best to help them.

In short, your clients want to be accepted as human beings, rather than be judged and evaluated as to whether they are right or wrong. They are not asking that you agree on all of their decisions, only that you be enthusiastic about getting the job done. They want you to look at their actions and suggestions to see if you think they will work. If you think they won't, then they want your support in figuring out some that will work.

Clients hope you will be generally sympathetic with the ups and downs in their work and personal life. They want you to be an effective communicator, with both written and verbal skills. They want you to be able to organize a statistical consulting session effectively so that the time is efficiently used.

You are not a statistical vending machine. Statistical consultation involves a relationship. Two or more people are working together to solve a problem. Thus, you will have use for many interpersonal skills.

THE STATISTICAL COMMUNITY'S NEEDS

This book is directed at statisticians whose jobs depend on satisfied clients; so we assume you care what your clients want. There is another group whose approval you seek: the statistical community.

Your client expects you to have the approval of your peers, just as you expect your doctor to be licensed to practice or your teachers to be peer approved. You like hearing from other doctors that your doctor is good. You like hearing from other teachers that your teacher is well respected in the field.

You can probably already see a problem developing. You know enough about medicine and academia to realize that a doctor's doctor doesn't necessarily have satisfied patients. The most prestigious professors (in the eyes of their peers) are not necessarily the best teachers. The conflict of peer approval versus client approval is not something clients or statisticians like to think about. It's very upsetting. One place to see the conflict between client approval and peer approval is in the continual financial battles of state universities. The taxpayers of the state (clients) want to hear that their state university "ranks very high." They also want to hear that its teachers are very good, that it's friendly in atmosphere, and that it does good community works for the state. These wants are in conflict. Universities are rated by other university professors (peers) according to the national research prestige of their faculties. The number of Nobel Prize winners on the faculty is important in counting points, but a Nobel Prize winner can't be available to all the students who want to take classes or have fireside chats. Nobel Prize winners have to be selfish about their time. Their classes are taught by their graduate students, who desperately seek their approval. They don't get their approval by teaching well; they get it by showing research potential.

Does the same problem exist in statistics? Yes. Behaving in a way to maximize approval of the statistics community does not maximize approval from clients. Behaving in a manner that maximizes client approval does not maximize statistician approval. Does seeking the approval of both clients and other statisticians put the consulting statistician in total conflict? No, but there's enough conflict to make you worry and give you a floating anxiety about how to do your job well. Let's look at the values of the statistical community by first looking at mathematics.

The Mathematics Community's Values

The fields of application of statistics vary widely, including natural sciences, laboratory sciences, clinical behavioral fields, and business. Those fields of application are so diverse that few statisticians are knowledgeable about all of them. Statisticians have one field of knowledge other than statistics in common, however: mathematics.

Even the least mathematically inclined statistician is good at arithmetic. To obtain the equivalent of a master's degree in statistics, a student must have at least a year of calculus, up through multiple integration, and some matrix algebra. For a Ph.D. in mathematical statistics, advanced probability theory (based on measure theory) is appropriate. The competent mathematical statistician has to be able to follow complicated proofs of theorems in mathematics and prove some on his or her own.

We statisticians are all very conscious of some of the contributions of mathematicians to our discipline. It's hard to imagine where applied statistics would be without the Central Limit Theorem, a profound result even in its simplest form. Understanding its proof and those of other limit theorems requires understanding mathematical analysis well beyond that of the typical calculus student. The creators of such theorems have to be excellent mathematicians. Statistics is deeply indebted to mathematics.

There is a key concept in mathematics that is admirable and enviable, but that distinguishes it sharply from the practice of statistics. In proving mathematical theorems, one has the hope of doing something that is absolutely correct. Some proofs of a theorem are more elegant than others, but they are all "correct." Almost never in applied statistics, however, can the practitioner attain the satisfaction of having done something unarguably right. Mathematics can never totally support the hard decisons of a practicing consultant. The consultant is on his or her own to decide whether n is large enough, or whether the population is not too skewed. Theoretical studies of the robustness of statistical data analysis techniques are either based on Monte Carlo methods or complicated mathematical analysis but cannot treat all distributions that arise in practice. The consultant knows very well that the parent distribution of the population from which the data is drawn is not exactly like one ever studied before.

The statistical consultant has to make the leap on his or her own, without benefit of mathematical theorems to assuage all doubts. Yet the beauty and precision of mathematics are clear in the conscience of the consultant, who always wants to be precise and clear and unarguably correct. The values of the mathematical community are ever present in the consultant's mind.

The Statistical Community's Values

The values of the statistical community are different from the values of the mathematical community, but there are some important similarities. The most noticeable one is our emphasis on quantitative intelligence. This is very natural because our field is so mathematical. There are professors at colleges and universities who call themselves statisticians but do not consult. We statisticians appreciate brilliance and compete with each other in a running intellectual contest, just like the mathematicians.

It looks like some prejudices may be softening. Recent articles by Marquardt (1980, 1981), Joiner (1980), Hunter (1981), and Snee et al. (1980) indicate the importance of being able to work effectively with scientists in other disciplines. A major theme presented by all these authors is that statistical expertise alone is not enough. To be effective, one must be able to take this expertise into the world and use it in collaboration with scientists from other disciplines.

We know of no study by sociologists or psychologists about statisticians. Sociologists and psychologists say that statisticians are interesting and should be studied. We have power over those two fields in that sociologists and psychologists intimidate each other by using statistics. It's hard to imagine their doing studies about us, the methodology of which we wouldn't criticize severely. An academic psychiatrist friend of ours says psychiatrists go crazy when anyone tries to study them. While we wait for the perfect study to be done on us, we'll have to settle for our own perceptions.

The reason for learning about the values of our field is that they have powerful influence on you. Departure from these values is a source of work anxiety. It's good to understand them.

There are several ways to observe the statistical community. One is to observe statisticians as people in various social and professional gatherings. Another is to recall the main messages of your statistics teachers. A third is to summarize the general impression you get from reading journals. From all these sources, two points are made loud and clear, over and over again:

1. The more you know, the better.

2. You can't be too careful.

These two canons are the rallying cries of statistics. To speak out or act out against them in public is to sin and thus invoke the wrath of the statistical community. It's easy for statistics professors to say these things, but the consultant trying to make a living in Corporation X has to compromise constantly.

Don't feel guilty if it takes you years to adjust to the dilemma of trying simultaneously to "please" academic statisticians and your nonacademic employer. The conflict, though painful, is a fact of life for every conscientious practitioner. The pain of it goes away with your aging.

SUMMARY

• Your clients want you to be technically competent, interested in helping them solve their problems, and able to relate to them as individuals.

• Your clients want you to be a good business manager, able to manage time and money. Sometimes they also want you to arrange for keypunching, coding, and programming.

• The statistical community wants you to advance the knowledge and prestige of statistics.

• The statistical community wants you to resist client pressures to compromise "too much."

• The statistical community is increasing its emphasis on statistical consulting.

CHAPTER 4

The Ideal Consultant

The committee of nine on training the industrial statistician chaired by Snee et al. (1980, p. 67) includes five members who are industrial statisticians. It offers a list of twelve attributes of an effective industrial statistician. "Effective" is much too modest, in our opinion. Anybody who can do all twelve well is ideal. Let's take a look at the list. The effective (or ideal) industrial statistician

1. Is well trained in the theory and practice of statistics
2. Is an effective problem solver
3. Has good oral and written communication skills
4. Can work within the constraints of the real world
5. Knows how to use computers to solve problems
6. Is familiar with the statistical literature

7. Understands the realities of statistical practice
8. Has a pleasing personality and is able to work with others
9. Gets highly involved in the solution of company problems
10. Is able to extend and develop statistical methodology
11. Can adapt quickly to new problems and challenges
12. Produces high-quality work in a timely fashion

We agree that all these attributes are relevant. It's a fine set. Nothing is left out. But it raises one giant question: "What are you going to do with this list?" It probably intimidates you. It intimidates us. (By the way, we are not industrial statisticians. We are professors in universities in departments of biometry and statistics. However, our identities in our universities are largely as consultants. We do consulting, teach it, give talks about it, and publish papers about it. Boen directs the Biometry Consulting Laboratory at the University of Minnesota. It's self-supporting and is a source of education and support for graduate students. All clients pay for service; no free work is done for any students and very little for faculty. Clients have to be satisfied or the Biometry Consulting Laboratory will fail. He also has a small extramural consulting practice. Zahn works in the Statistical Consulting Center at Florida State University and has a much larger private consulting practice.)

APPLYING THE LIST

Let's go over the list, item by item. Boen will grade himself on each.

Training

(1) Is well trained in the theory and practice of statistics. I know *about* most of the areas of applied statistics, but some of my knowledge is terribly skimpy. I've tried a few times to learn about time series and factor analysis, but

never got around to it. I certainly can't do them. The fact is, I just avoid those areas. I refer a client who needs time series help to another statistician. As for clients who demand factor analysis, I first try to talk them out of it. If I can't do that, I refer. As to how *well trained* I am in the theory and practice of statistics, I don't know how to answer.

Solving Problems

(2) Is an effective problem solver. I'm definitely in favor of being an effective problem solver. I hope I am one. I know I'm not effective for every client, having messed up a few, making them worse instead of better. Sometimes I've told my colleagues what I did for such and such a client and been told my solutions were dumb. Sometimes they were praised. Most of my clients thank me and pay their bill. Many times I think I've been clever and made a silk purse out of a sow's ear (this is much easier if you start with a silk sow), and the client has been absolutely rescued from a disaster, whether he knows it or not. Frankly, I think I'm pretty good at problem solving, depending on how you define the problem. Maybe everybody thinks they're good at problem solving.

If there's anything hard to get straight, it's what the problem really is. You could say about a client's problem that the *problem* is one of getting *something* done. You could also say that the *problem* is one of fitting a good model. It must be like the blind men feeling an elephant, with distinctly different perceptions of the men feeling different parts. Everybody thinks they're logical, too.

Communicating

(3) Has good oral and written communication skills. How are you at these? I enjoy oral more than written communication. Oral is less work; I can watch people's reaction and listen to their tone of voice. It's much more sociable, which I like.

One of the big questions in consulting is what should be put in writing? We'll deal with that later. The question here is how good do you have to be to get high marks as a consultant. We rate communication skills as being very important in consulting, particularly with respect to the emphasis given it in most master's programs in statistics. It's even become a new motherhood, with everybody saying that we need more communication around here. Communications is one of the skills at which everybody thinks they're good, particularly if others would just pay attention.

The question for you is whether you should work on your communication skills, which implicitly requires you to ask if you are good enough already, and, if you're not, what are the costs and benefits of trying to improve.

Facing Reality

(4) Can work within the constraints of the real world. This is a vital competency. We all have *some* difficulty with harsh realities (for example, the imminence of our own death), but one problem certain to break the most gifted statistician-scientist who wants to consult is the stark reality of the consultant's real world. These realities include constraints of time, money, personalities, and company politics.

Using Computers

(5) Knows how to use computers to solve problems. This depends on your situation and whether you do the computing or you get someone else to do it. It's vital that it be done, and done well. I don't know how to program, but I get it done by people who work for me. We'll talk later about arranging for coding, keypunching, and programming.

Keeping Current

(6) Is familiar with the statistical literature. This is an area of guilt and anxiety for me. I'm just not keeping up. It seems hopeless, with all the new statistics papers being published. I read the tables of contents in *Biometrics, Journal of the ASA,* and the *American Statistician.* I usually read some book reviews, a couple of letters to the editors, and some

nontechnical papers in the *American Statistician.* I try to understand the essence of one paper a month, but I don't actually *study* technical papers anymore. Maybe I will again someday, but right now I'm burned out.

Understanding Reality

(7) Understands the realities of statistical practice. I think I do. Otherwise, where would I get the gall to write this book?

Congeniality

(8) Has a pleasing personality and is able to work with others. My answer is no and yes. There are people who like my personality, but they are either of high ego strength or insensitive. I do well in some long-term relationships, but my personality is not pleasing. I really turn some people off, particularly those who need continual reassurance. As for working with people, I am so-so. There are several people I intimidate. If I *work at it,* I can reassure even the most frightened person in the short run. It's amazing how well some of the new psychology techniques work, even when I'm in a bad mood and have to get along with a client, a peer, or my family.

Getting Involved

(9) Gets highly involved in the solution of company problems. I occasionally get very involved, but generally not. Most of my consultation is "quick and dirty." I prefer it as a life-style, with a wide variety of people and situations. Some of my colleagues give me a hard time for being a shallow consultant, though, and I have attacks of guilt on this point. I get defensive and tell them that if I got "very involved" with every client, there'd be many potential clients who would never see a statistician. I think people are either deep or broad, depending on their personality. I won't change unless put under great pressure.

Contributions to the Field

(10) Is able to extend and develop statistical methodology. I've done some of it. Professors are under the gun to do it, as it should be. Maybe I did just enough to get promoted and tenured. I'm not that interested in it anymore. I've fallen behind in the journals so badly that most of my ideas turn out to be already known, published about forty years ago. As for new statistical methodology for clients, I've been terribly burned. I used to cook up some new analyses for their data, but I scared the clients to death. They were very honest. They wanted tried and true methods that they wouldn't have to defend.

I tried it again last year, using a "better" analysis. The client had a funny look on his face, but went along with it even though it cost him more money. He even came around to liking it, until he sent his results to a journal and got them soundly rejected. The editor and referees had never heard of the method. They insisted that a straight line be fit, instead of my fancy, monotonic, bounded curve with maximum likelihood estimates. The client forgave me, but I pouted for a few days and resolved again to use only standard procedures on clients.

Adaptability

(11) Can adapt quickly to new problems and challenges. It depends on what is meant. I think I'm pretty good at this and actually thrive on it. I get bored easily and like new ideas and situations, given that the latter aren't too traumatic.

Promptness and Quality

(12) Produces high-quality work in a timely fashion. I think it's on time for the most part. Being on time is something I take pride in. Now for the high-quality part. It's not bad, overall, but it certainly could be of higher quality. I usually avoid writing a report for the client when I can. The real reason is a combination of laziness and trying to do too many things.

APPLYING THE LIST TO YOU

How were your grades? I give myself four As, three Cs, and the rest Bs, and I've been consulting for eighteen years. I expect to remain inadequate in several areas, partly due to lack of ability, lack of ambition, and some deep-seated character and personality shortcomings.

Everyone is uneven in their strengths. By now, your character and personality are pretty well set. They are subject to change with major life events, but in the short run you are what you are, and that's it. The problem is somehow to maximize the use of the raw material—you—to become the best statistical consultant you can.

It's up to you to choose your goals. The twelve competencies compiled by the Snee committee make a fine, comprehensive list. The consulting bibliography of Woodward and Schucany (1977) contains thirty-seven papers, many written by active, well-respected consultants. Each of them wrote his or her own views of what's important in consultation. There is definitely some difference of opinion among those authors. Daniel (1969) puts mathematical statistical knowledge as the fourth most important competence for a consultant, preceded by scientific background *of the consultant,* attitude and general manner toward technical people, and experience with real data and real experiments, in that order. Daniel says the better consultant enjoys cooperative enterprise and has little need to be dominant. He particularly cautions against brashness, arrogance, and imperiousness. Another consultant, Marquardt (1979) emphasizes the importance of total project involvement to statisticians who want recognition in their company.

After reading all we could find of the statistical consulting literature, we arrived at the following conclusions:

1. The more mathematics, statistics, computing, and science you know, the better.
2. Academic knowledge of the four subjects is not enough. There is a separate skill of *applying* that knowledge. Every author says experience is necessary to develop it.

3. There is more to consulting than having and applying knowledge. Attitudes toward client and self are important. Business matters enter in.

Of the three broad categories—technical knowledge, skill in its application, and people and business problems— you already know how to achieve the first. It comes from academic activity like studying books, talking, attending courses, reading journals, and publishing papers. In other words, it's what colleges and universities do. At your graduation ceremony, somebody gave a stirring commencement address telling you, among other things, to keep studying. You already have several books and can buy more. You can subscribe to more journals, too. Everybody who's gone through college knows what this is and how to do it. *Whether* you do it, as a graduate, is up to you.

The second category, applying that knowledge, is learned by experience. Most beginning statisticians need supervision under a seasoned practitioner. What we mean by application skill is things like choosing an analysis for a messy problem. (When you didn't design it yourself, the problem is always messy.) You can think of three ways to do it, each with various strengths and weaknesses, including robustness, explainability to the client, and acceptability to the statistical community. Except for getting a lot of experience, there's no agreed-upon way to learn it. There certainly is such a thing as talent for doing it. We're convinced temperament plays a key role. To *enjoy* doing it requires a *modified* perfectionism; it's doing your best in the face of many restrictions, without an anxiety attack. The good applier is clever at making do with the tools at hand. In this book, we shall touch on the skill of application, but we shall not tackle directly the problem of precisely what analysis to use for particular consulting problems. We avoid advising you just what analysis to perform for what messy problems because we have no particular wisdom to offer and, by its very nature, the "just what to do" for real problems will always be the central topic of applied statistics, one destined for endless debate. There will always be the conflict of philosophical differences of parametric versus nonparametric, questions of the utility of hypothesis testing, whether to use decision theory, and so on. These issues are going to stay hot and unsettled for the forseeable future. In illustrating points by examples from our practices, we shall roughly describe what analysis we did. We know full well that our having done it does not make it "correct." As a matter of fact, one of our main points is that there is never a unique correct solution to a real problem. The effective consultant has to face that fact.

The focus of this book is the third part of consulting—the business and people problems. We do stick our necks out, in a directive manner, and offer some specific principles for consultation. They are *extremely* practical.

SUMMARY

• There are plenty of jobs for statistical consultants who fall short of the ideal.

• You can't know everything.

• You're going to make mistakes.

• Hang in there and keep plugging.

CHAPTER 5

Choosing a Technique: The Practical Aspects

In America's state of advanced technology, there are many examples of heroic rescues using incredibly complicated machinery and techniques. Helicopters rescue stranded mountain climbers; surgeons fix brains and replace organs; and hypnotists cure smokers. The amazing number of cures achieved by "take two aspirins and go to bed" gets little newspaper coverage. We have come to expect rescue by new, exciting, awe-inspiring techniques in situations that drip with drama. This explains clients' expectations that statistical consultants can do wonderful and mysterious things to huge data sets, no matter how badly collected.

In addition to their expectation of a flashy rescue, we have our own forces driving us to use complicated techniques. As a student, you were always pushed into learning more difficult concepts and procedures. It was hard work, but you felt very satisfied when you learned how to create an ANOVA table for a two-way layout. You and your teacher were very proud of you. (Your teacher may not have shown it; statistics teachers don't give lavish praise.) After getting a few techniques like ANOVA under your belt, ones that clients can't do by themselves, it's very tempting to show your client that you know how to do it. This isn't all bad, because the client wants to believe that we know everything about statistics. There is another force pushing us to use complicated techniques. The mathematical statistical community is building new techniques and refining old ones at a rapid rate and is anxious to see them used. Thus, if you seek the approval of the mathematical statistical community (we all do, to some extent), you'll be tempted to use new, complicated techniques. In addition, some clients want to intimidate their audiences, not inform them, with complicated techniques.

TECHNIQUES TO USE

In spite of all the pressures on statisticians to use new, fancy techniques, there are some compelling practical reasons to stay away from them. It is a purpose of this chapter to make the case, in consulting, for preferring simple techniques and fundamental concepts. (What is "simple" will vary widely, depending on the statistical consultant, the client, and the context.) Actually, you play an invaluable role in consultation by "simply" helping your clients to clarify their research objectives. Questions such as "What would you hope to answer by performing that analysis?" or "How will you know if you have answered that question?" lead the client to set goals that are achievable.

Here is an example to illustrate what we mean by choosing a simple technique: A client came for advice on analyzing data already collected for studying the relationships between the education of women and contraceptive use in Nepal. He said he wanted to use multiple regression to search for predictors of contraceptive use. The eleven predictor variables are mostly dichotomous or or trichotomous, with a couple of them being quantitative discrete (such as number of visits to relatives per year). After some discussion, I began to see that the trichotomous variables were not as conspicuously ordered as the client had said they were. They were questions like "Woman is read newspaper, by husband or father." Three possible answers are no, by husband, and by father. I pushed for dichotomization into "is read newspaper" versus "is not read newspaper" because neither "husband" nor "father" is clearly more educating. I then got the client to dichotomize the quantitative discrete variables so that *all* the derived predictor variables were dichotomous, with one of the values clearly desired. (It is more desired to be read the newspaper than not to have access to a newspaper.) I got him to do the dichotomizing, fully aware that in so doing we were throwing away information, particularly on the quantitative discrete variables. The point of this story is that sometimes we choose to use simpler techniques in order to make points clearer even though we know there is some information loss.

Statistician Understanding

It's one thing to learn how to do a t-test; it's another thing to know when to do it and what it means. We teach many service courses to students who are forced to take statistics. Most learn *how* to do a t-test, although not many memorize the formula. Those who do memorize the formula forget it quickly after the course is over. In these service courses, we try to cover the concept of power, but it's really too hard a concept for them to understand and we try to teach it mainly for our own sense of completeness. Many service course teachers don't even attempt it. Many of our clients have this level of background in statistics.

Furthermore, if the t-test is one-sided, it is the optimal (uniformly most powerful) test. Even if the assumptions were all satisfied exactly (a practical impossibility in a real situation), you could still do other tests, like a Mann-Whitney. *Now* I know that (1) the assumptions for optimality do not have to be at all true for one to be able to do the t-test and (2) even if they were all true, there are still other tests to do.

Because they can't be exactly true in practice, it's not clear which you should use, the t-test or the Mann-Whitney. After all, the Mann-Whitney is more powerful than the t-test for certain parent distributions, and you can't even practicably find out what the two-parent distributions are. In addition to all this uncertainty as to whether to use the t-test or the Mann-Whitney, the α-level is arbitrary. What the α-level *should* be (aside from the overwhelming pressure by clients to use .05 for every situation) depends on the costs of the type I and type II errors. Furthermore, there's the question of whether *any* test is appropriate. Perhaps the appropriate goal of the analysis is estimation, which raises the issue of what to estimate: the difference of population means or the difference of population medians?

We now know a great deal about the t-test, particularly its robustness. We can tell others how to do it, have some good guidelines as to when to do it, can compare to other plausible techniques, know it's robust with respect to type I errors, and know what it means when it's done. We can also look at a couple of sets of numbers and see if the results make sense, as well as "explain" to a client *why* it was or wasn't statistically significant. In summary, we feel on top of the t-test.

Multiple regression is another matter. We've used it dozens of times and know a fair amount about its properties, but there's still a lot we don't know. It's been covered in many texts and hundreds of papers, the great majority of which we haven't read. There's also much client pressure to use it. In certain situations, like searching for subsets of predictor variables, it's really the only technique available. What makes us nervous is our ignorance of its robustness in the face of all kinds of distributions of predictor variables. Some predictor variables are dichotomous with very unsymmetrical distributions and with all levels of correlations among them. The multivariate distribution among them must be a long way from normal. We know there are papers published on the topic that we should read and know we should explore thoroughly with Monte Carlo studies the underlying parent distributions in this case, but time and money are ever-present consulting realities. We just don't know everything and are behind in the literature. So, we do what we have to do with what we have at the time. With multiple regression, searching for some subset of predictor variables, we're pretty uncertain. We are much more confident of our understanding of some techniques than others and, when given a choice, lean toward making do with the techniques we understand well. This attitude is appropriate for consulting and opposes absolutely the desire to use more complicated techniques in order to practice using them.

Client Acceptance

In choosing among techniques, it is very desirable to use one that the client accepts and is used to. How much to cater to clients is a major controversy in the field of statistics. At one extreme is the view that clients are like children with no judgment, that it is up to us to decide what is best for them and that we should insist on doing the right statistical thing. At the other extreme is the view that the customer is always right and the consultant's role is simply to clarify the client's instructions and then carry them out. Bross (1974) articulated the two positions, calling the issue "scientist and shoe clerk." This issue of how much say the client should have is a topic of debate for every profession. If you want a lively discussion, ask doctors how many patients know what's good for them or ask teachers about the wisdom of catering to student requests. This issue of choosing a technique for client pleasing is a key one in statistical consulting. Before plunging into it, let's warm up by looking at some medical situations.

There are medical situations in which it is out of the question for the patient to participate in decision making. The unconscious accident victim, going into shock as he is checked into the emergency room, is in no shape to co-decide on his treatment. There are other situations, however, in which the patient's understanding of the treatment is vital for the treatment. An eighty-one-year-old man acts as though he's starting to become senile. His physician prescribed a medicine to be taken for five days straight, but to do the five-day regimen once a month. The man keeps getting under-doses and overdoses because he forgets when he last had a five-day session. He says he would remember it easily if he took the medicine every day.

In statistical consulting, unlike in medicine, we never have strictly passive clients. Clients have to *do something*. Usually, they have to defend the statistical analysis to somebody. According to Hyams (1971, p. 209), "The consultant should not offer solutions that are beyond the comprehension of the experimenter or his ability to describe them." What analyses can most clients understand? We are very pessimistic about how much clients understand of what we do. The only analysis many clients and their audiences understand is a simple graph. Hyams's point is very strong, and we support it in principle. We don't always adhere to it because some clients' statistical ability simply is not enough for them to understand even the least complicated analysis.

I did one analysis that was a little nonstandard. I was so proud of it. Everything came out beautifully linear on the bivariate graph if both variables were logged, but I just couldn't get the client to understand logs. I respected him for being so sincere and honest, but we were both very frustrated. Two one-hour sessions of talking, trying to explain why logging both variables was good and why Pearson's *r* was inappropriate for the problem didn't make a dent. The client stuck to his guns and pooled all the data for the several subjects into one graph, and I claimed they needed separate graphs. The client understood graphs, but not logs. This is an illustration of how little some clients understand; that client holds a Ph.D. in a basic science.

There are several psychological rewards available to statistical consultants. One of our favorite rewards is the sight and sound of a client who lights up with a flash of insight about the data. It's nice to see clients happy because we did something fancy that gets results they wanted, but we feel much more satisfied if the analysis we suggest is something they *understand*. Clients are forever grateful for the simple graph that makes their data crystal clear to them. Clients are delighted with an official analysis that's also a presentation to their peers. The simple graph, when appropriate, is a major consulting virtue. Often it's all you need. Consultants who worry that their analysis isn't complicated enough to impress mathematical statisticians have a problem. This brings up an essential point about consulting: Effective consultants very seldom in their consulting do things that impress mathematical statisticians. Mathematical statisticians are on the lookout for new mathematical statistical concepts or the use of previously unused techniques. It's good for consulting statisticians to develop new mathematical statistical techniques, but they should avoid using them just to exercise a new mathematical statistical idea at the client's expense.

Problems with New Techniques.   If you use too new a technique, the client's field will have a hard time accepting it. This creates an uphill battle for the clients who can't refer to other researchers in the field that have used and thus legitimized it. I ruined a consulting relationship with two clients. They met me as far as they could, but I pushed the new (to their field) technique too hard. Here's the story.

The clients were two physicians who specialized in internal medicine. I had known the older one, a man in his fifties, for a few years. He's outgoing and is a forceful person with high ego strength. His associate was a woman about thirty. She was not forceful, but very conscientious and persistent in her research. The essence of the problem was the establishment of a "normal" range for a bivariate distribution of blood gases in healthy children. The researcher's goal was to agree with a paper published by other researchers who had established a bivariate distribution of medical normalcy on a different group of subjects.

My difficulty was that the previous authors had presented their bivariate tolerance region in the wrong way. They had calculated the least squares regression line of one of the blood gas variables, Y, on the other one, X. They had made a parallelogram by going up and down 2 $s_{y \cdot x}$ from the regression line and going left and right 2 s_x from $\bar{x}$. A postdoctoral fellow working with me quickly spotted that it should be a tolerance ellipsoid, with a fatter middle and smaller ends. He was right. The bivariate scatterplot looked bivariate normal enough to do it; so I started to try to sell the clients on it.

My suggestion to do an analysis different from what the other paper had done troubled them. I said I could do what the other authors had done, but I didn't think it was nearly as correct a procedure. The physicians assured me they wanted to do the right statistical thing, but wondered what was wrong with the predecessor's parallelogram. I went through my explanation as best I could in every way I knew how. They tried to get it, but couldn't. They discussed it with their colleagues and said their colleagues thought they ought to do it with a parallelogram solely because the previous paper had. I tried the appeal that they could be statistical heroes by championing a new (to their field) technique and introduce something statistically better. That attracted them a little, but the fear of trying something statistically new was too great. I had the data analyzed both ways for them, and they saw it really made a difference. In the end, however, I lost. They published it with the established, parallelogram method. All this activity cost them much time and money (my time with them cost them money). When I ran into them subsequently in the hall and asked them what had taken place, they were polite but disappointed in me. Putting it as gently as they could, they said they wasted a lot of money and indirectly asked why I couldn't have just done it the way they wanted it in the first place. It would have been much cheaper for them, they said. I had to agree.

That was too bad. Both they and I felt bad after it was all over. All those sessions took about five weeks and their statistical bill was too high for their small research budget. I knew they had meant well, as I had, but something went wrong. I'm still unsettled about it, half thinking it was my ethical duty and half thinking I was just plain naive and stupid. Looking back, if I had to do it over again and two methods had given more similar answers, I wouldn't make such a fuss. Have I learned something from it? I wonder about myself sometimes. I did it again since then, spending a lot of a client's time and money to come up with an analysis the journal wouldn't accept. The journal insisted the client find a statistician to do it the established way, fitting a straight line. I used another functional form that required expensive maximum likelihood estimation. In this latter case, the client sympathized with me and felt I was right. Subsequently, this client came back to me with another problem in which he wanted to use a more mathematically sophisticated analysis, but was getting flak from his counterparts in England. We commiserated with each other for a while, but I wound up talking him out of the sophisticated analysis. It would over-emphasize the statistical point and delay scientific progress.

Data Collection and Design.   One area in which client understanding and acceptance of your advice is absolutely essential is in design. Occasionally, clients do their own analy-sis without your supervision, thus making it particularly important that they understand how to do it, but most of the time you will do the analysis. Thus, the analysis is usually much more under your control than the enforcing of the design. The conscientious statistician can recommend a com-plicated design and then hover over the client to make sure it is done right. (Hovering takes your time, however, and may not be something you like to do. It also may not be some-thing your clients like having done to them.) There are cost-benefit questions about whether to use complicated designs in that you must spend time monitoring complicated designs.

Even if you want to spend your time monitoring a de-sign, though, and the client welcomes you doing so, it is sometimes impossible to do it thoroughly. There are some-times too many decisions made by people who are unscien-tific and uncommitted to the study, as illustrated by the following case.

I'm the senior statistician on a large, multifaceted study of ear infection. One part of it is experimental laboratory work with animals. The other part of the study is observa-tional on surgical patients. In the latter part, the adult pa-tients are given forms to fill out about their ear health history; the pediatric forms are filled out by patients' moth-ers or whoever else brings them to the clinic. The patients are not scientists. They just want treatment. In addition, there is much data to be collected by doctors and audiolo-gists on still more forms.

At first blush, you might ask what this task has to do with a statistician. Can't the doctors and audiologists do this themselves? Not in this case. They don't have enough experience in clinical research. In the form design stage, which lasted several weeks, I pushed the senior investigators very hard to make the questionnaires ones that ordinary people, hurting and in waiting rooms, could answer by themselves. The physicians, however, thought of all kinds of things they want to know about the patients. They desperately wanted to know details of their history, like when the patients had ear infection episodes and what antibiotics they had taken.

I insisted they were asking for all kinds of information they couldn't obtain. Many patients don't know what antibiotics they used to take or remember the dates of the ear events. It is easy for physicians to overestimate the cooperation of patients. When they are *with* a patient, the patient seems to the doctor to want to cooperate. Even patients who bitterly resent doctors as a species are very cooperative with their doctor. The patient in the waiting room has a very different attitude about cooperation in filling out a *research* form. If they read and understand the consent form they sign, they see that filling out the history form is for *research* and will not be even seen by their doctor. Then their motivation is entirely different. Why should they bother with trying conscientiously to recall their own history? The only hope at all was to make the questionnaire *extremely* easy. This meant much work, pretesting and all, to boil it down to the point of incredible simplicity and ease for the respondent. It's been working pretty well, with good patient compliance for one year on several hundred patients.

The beginning consultant may say, "Is it the statistician's role to get down to that level, to even help doctors write questionnaires?" Yes! Making that questionnaire simple was the only hope of getting some decent patient history data. It was not possible financially to get someone to help patients recall their history. The study wasn't funded to cover that. The choice was either to get patient history data from the patient or not get it at all. I talked with the investigators at length about not getting it at all, but they decided to try to get some of it and gave up on obtaining the names of antibiotics taken in the past. All most people know about their medicine is that they're taking pills. Most don't even know whether they had an ear infection in the past, unless a physician told them so. They just remember that their ear hurt. They don't look in their own ears; so if pus doesn't run out, they don't know if there's pus in them. Some patients are very sophisticated, of course, knowing what antibiotics they took when, but we went for the lowest common denominator. Many of the patients in the study were disadvantaged and conspicuously uneducated.

What are some morals of this story? One is that helping with the patient history questionnaire was part of my role, not because somebody said it was, but because it had to be done and nobody else could or would do it. We don't have to decide whether it was "statistical." If it wasn't done right at the level of questionnaire design, the history portion was going to fail. It was going to fail if it wasn't extremely simple because there was nobody to monitor it. A moral is that it was a design issue, and practical limitations didn't allow for monitoring. The data came from the patients' minds, and nobody could hover over those patients to make them do it better. There wasn't the money to pay someone to do it, and it wouldn't have worked if there had been.

The story raises a key issue. Can you orient yourself so that your purpose is parallel to the client's purpose of getting the job done, in the sense we used in Chapter 2? Can you be counted on to be responsible for getting the job done? Developing a reputation for being responsible will yield great future dividends.

This ear infection project had other problems in the human subjects studied. Perhaps "design" is a misleading word, and we should say "data collection" instead. Design may connote to you only the narrower image of deciding whether to use a completely randomized allocation or a randomized block allocation, but the appreciated statistician is one who uses all his or her wits, wherever possible, to make the study work. In more data collection planning for the ear infection study, there were forms to design on which physicians were to record their observations made during surgery. The ear surgeons, mostly residents, were already overworked and resented filling out forms for somebody else's research project. Most residents aren't interested in research anyway. They were taking the forms home at night and trying to recall what they saw during surgery. There was too much detail to remember, even when they could discipline themselves to do it. Luckily, the study had money for a "secretary" to be in the operating room and fill out the form according to the surgeons' verbal reports of their observations. This worked well. I didn't need to solve this problem because someone else did, but solving this kind of very practical problem is worth its weight in gold in building client confidence in statistician involvement.

In these examples of design for data collection on the ear infection study, my input was vital. Because I know that big nonresponse problems are statistically devastating in inference, I was able to push, persuade, cajole, and bully them into a data collection plan that would have a low nonresponse rate. Notice the distinction between pushing for the simple plan for reasons of tidiness and completeness and insisting on it for reasons of inferences. Only a statistician can effectively justify the latter. It is simplicity for a statistical purpose.

CHECKING RESULTS

There are other reasons for using simple techniques with which you are familiar, in addition to your being able to understand them better and your clients not having to defend them to their audiences. If the technique is an analysis you have used several times before, you have probably learned how to check whether the calculations are correct. The importance of this cannot be overemphasized. It hasn't happened often recently, but we've really been embarrassed because of calculation errors in things we've given to clients. The amount of our embarrassment has ranged from negligible to beet red. The seriousness of consequences spanned the whole spectrum also. Sometimes we've caught our mistakes during an evening of afterthought and frantically tried to reach the client at home. When that failed, it was a long night waiting to reach him or her in the morning. Sometimes we miss the errors out of our own laziness or are too busy and rushed. Other times it is due to the complexity of what we have done and there just isn't a convenient check on accuracy. Notice how our behavior conflicts with the "shoulds" of statistics.

The best check on calculations is to plot the data and see if the model fits. This is easy if the predictor variable is one dimensional, but not if the predictor variable is many dimensional. A tough case is that of the multicelled contingency table when the end point is a p-value or some association coefficient. We worry when doing something a little over our head conceptually or hard to check. The danger of making mistakes is greatest on the quick-and-dirty consultation. We do several of them, but stick close to very simplest of techniques to lessen our error rate.

One last advantage of using simple, familiar techniques is your ability to estimate the time and money required to do the work. It is very advantageous to use familiar packaged programs over having to write new programs or even specifying many parameters in the all-purpose program. Once you're into writing a new computer program for a complicated statistical analysis, time and cost estimates are extremely rough. A few years ago, we tried to find at the University of Minnesota a program for a split plot design. That took several weeks of searching around the university program sources, calling and writing letters to people outside, trying to find a package that would do split plots and be compatible with our computer. Side issues included faculty arguments (probably good for us) about why we don't have that program in our shop. However, the client didn't enjoy this lively debate one bit. It is a better policy to use analyses, when you can, that don't require new analysis programs to be written.

CLIENT PARTICIPATION AND UNDERSTANDING

There are two questions to be answered in choosing a technique, and their answers help determine what procedures are used. The first question is that of how much of the statistical work that is planned will be done by the client.

If the client will do it *all*, it must be at the level of the client's ability and resources. Clients' computational resources are commonly very limited, such as to a desk calculator. However, even in the "data hospital" model in which the client dumps the whole computation problem onto the statistical unit, the client may want to learn something about the statistical procedures. Whether or not this service of explanation is provided by the data hospital is a policy decision for the statistical unit.

The second question concerns the *amount* of the analysis clients need to understand and the *level of understanding* they need. The amount of client understanding necessary depends on the construction of the final report and how it will be presented to the client's supervisor and scientific colleagues. If clients are to write up the report and present it as a solo effort, then the analyses must be at a level that they can understand because they have to answer the questions the administrators and other scientists will ask pertaining to the statistical techniques used. It is risky to use tools beyond clients' levels of understanding in this situation. Report credibility will suffer and its impact will be lessened if clients have to interrupt the flow of the presentation either to delay questions for a later time or to take a very tentative guess at answering a question that is beyond them. In short, if you aren't going to be there for the report presentation, your clients must be able to present your work. To ascertain that they are, you need to quiz your clients tactfully about their understanding and ability to present the material. Although we stress the need for tact, we have sensed no resentment if clients are informed as to the purpose. The key is to convey the fact that you are both being judged in their presentation and that you are "in it together."

Ideally, you will be involved in the final report on the client's project (but you probably won't be unless you negotiate it). Regardless of which strategy is finally agreeable to both you and your client, it is ideal if you meet jointly, *before* writing the final draft, with your client and with the individuals who are consumers of the final report. Find out as much as you can about what they really want. Are they interested mainly in comparisons of males and females, or is the real interest in elaborate multiple regression modeling? Do they appear to be especially interested in graphic presentations? This meeting will show the statistical level of the report consumers, as well as the particular aspects of the problem that most interest them. You will find some of the report consumers unable or unwilling to be specific, but enough of them are typically helpful to make the meeting worthwhile.

If you are to collaborate with the client on the presentation, then the level of analysis should be one that you can explain and communicate to the nonstatisticians who are consumers of the report.

Political conditions can determine the collaboration issue. For example, a state-of-the-art analysis is commonly required in a new drug proposal to the FDA, and the statistical consultant must be a collaborator in the effort. The final report is otherwise in great peril.

If the client proposes a technique that is almost as good as one you can think of, compliment him or her. Unless yours is considerably better, don't even mention it. The one he or she thought of is one that your client probably understands and will thus use much more effectively. Don't worry that he or she will think you don't know statistics. Your supporting his or her solution is likely to give you a good client.

REPORTS TO CLIENTS

Principles of the Oral Report

Oral reports have some definite advantages over written reports, including immediate verbal and nonverbal feedback from the client. Immediate feedback permits you to clarify your report on the spot. To be sure you make best use of the oral method of reporting, keep in mind the following principles.

1. Watch your client's face when you give your report orally.

2. Let him interrupt your oral report at any point and any number of times. Encourage this. Ask questions that invite more than a yes or no answer to see if your communications have been successful.

3. Patiently answer any question or listen to any comment the client has regarding your report.

4. Accept undefensively any criticism of your work, although you should give reasons for difficulties that have occurred. See what can be done to make the report work better in this area.

5. If the client seems confused by your report, offer to hear his or her understanding of what you said. If the client still seems confused, offer to try writing your report or explaining it another time, whichever the client prefers.

Principles of the Written Report

Written reports have certain advantages over oral reports. Written reports are essentially permanent and difficult to modify after the fact. As a result, considerable thought should be given to this in preparation. We recommend keeping in mind the following principles.

1. Write a crude, rough, "sandpaper" draft as soon as possible, sooner than you think you are ready to start writing.

2. Avoid technical jargon as much as possible. If you want to include it to impress the client that you and your work are "deep" (sometimes advantageous to do), don't require that the reader understand the jargon. Tell the reader that the technical details are included only for completeness should another statistician want to read it and show exactly what reasoning and procedures you used.

3. Stay clear of a legalistic tone unless your relationship with the client is confrontive and legalistic. If not, make the tone friendly and helpful.

4. If at all appropriate, keep it short.

5. Give your phone number and encourage the client to call you with further comments or questions. (You may find that the client wants to ask; if so, encourage him or her to do so.)

6. Keep a copy of your report.

7. Think hard about to whom to send a copy. Check with the client as to who, if anyone, should receive a copy. Be prepared for the client to request that no one else receive a copy. If the client seems worried about a "leak," offer to give your report to him or her only orally.

SUMMARY

• Almost all clients want you to use techniques already accepted by their fields. In using a technique new to their fields, you are taking on a cause. Make sure it's worth it to your client.

• It's hard to make and meet deadlines when you use a technique new to you.

• Use the simplest technique that will do the job, not the fanciest you can handle.

• If the client's solution is decent, don't push your own unless it is much better. This strategy will most likely give you an ideal client in the long run.

• Be ready to help clients design data collection systems, including questionnaires.

• Work very hard for client understanding and acceptance of your ideas in the design.

• Agree how much of the work the client must do and/ or understand before choosing a technique.

• Get your purposes and intentions aligned with the client's. Be 100 percent responsible for getting your part of the job done. Let the client know if you cannot be counted on to participate in the study at this level.

• In giving oral reports, take full advantage of client feedback to clarify your presentation.

• Written reports are permanent. Prepare them carefully; use simple language and be clear and concise.

CHAPTER 6

The Target—
Your Client's Audience

You need to know the criteria by which your statistical consultation will be judged. It is necessary to consider these criteria if you are going to survive as a statistical consultant. Marquardt (1981) has offered a list of criteria by which a consultant may be judged. Conversations with Marquardt and other consultants in industry indicate that the critical facet of the evaluation is the impact of the final report on company operations. The bottom line is *impact*. Your choice depends on who is to be convinced and *how* they will be convinced. The analysis with the most impact is seldom the most mathematically sophisticated statistical analysis. Instead, it blends scientific rigor and insights into what are the political realities and traditions of the environment in which you are working. Simpler tools, explained carefully, will have a far more positive impact on the company than the most modern analysis that no one understands and therefore cannot appreciate. For example, it is especially important in cases that may involve litigation for the consultant to consider the consumer of the analysis, namely the *judge*, and how well he or she can understand what has been done.

BELIEVERS AND NONBELIEVERS

A consulting statistician facilitates communication between the client and the client's audience. It is vital to think about the client's audience and how that audience thinks. If the statistician doesn't help this communication, the statistician fails. If the client doesn't present the results to the audience in a manner comprehensible to that audience, the client fails. These are harsh but relevant facts. The client's audience may or may not believe in formal statistics; people often do *not* believe. In this chapter, we'll suggest strategies for nonbelievers as well as believers.

The essential distinction between believer and nonbeliever audiences of the client is that the former likes complicated statistical techniques and the latter distrusts them. The scientific audience typically likes advancing technology and sees complicated statistical technique as a form of advanced terminology. The unscientific audience may admire technology, but doesn't understand it. The unscientific audience doesn't understand any but the very simplest concepts of statistics (for example, mean and median, but not statistical tests). When an unscientific audience is persuaded by a statistical argument of any complexity (such as a χ^2 test), it is persuaded by statistical authority, and not by following statistical reasoning.

Your clients are often scientific with an unscientific audience. Your client's unscientific audience in industry or government consists of administrators. If the scientists and statisticians in a drug company recommend the production of a new drug, some vice-president is held responsible if the drug is manufactured, sold, and then brings an avalanche of lawsuits. Unscientific vice-presidents are not persuaded by their faith in the scientists and statisticians below them unless the arguments are extremely simple, such as scatter plots and tables of means. Statistical tests are just so much statistical jargon to them. Such audiences often think that fancy analyses are snow jobs.

THE ART OF PERSUASION

Convincing the Audiences

In helping scientists communicate statistically with their scientific peers, it is important to learn what statistical techniques they are used to. You should try to use techniques commonly used in their field. Different fields have different statistical traditions, with some using statistics and others avoiding statistics. Pharmacologists and experimental psychologists use statistics much more than chemists do. Further, some specialties use certain techniques. Engineers use control charts, but surgeons haven't heard of them. Experimental psychologists specialize in experimental designs and analysis of variance. Many epidemiologists know only χ^2 tests and use them constantly.

The idea here is very simple. If you're going to persuade people of something, the smartest thing you can do is find out *how* they get persuaded. As simple and compelling as this sounds and as true as it is, there is one difficulty. *Asking* people how they get persuaded doesn't usually evoke an honest, clear answer, for two reasons. The first is that it's difficult to know that about oneself. The second is that we in the statistical-scientific-industrial-governmental world try very hard to be viewed by others as rational. We are embarrassed by how emotional, illogical, and prejudiced we really are. We know we would be criticized if others knew our personal prejudices. You are observing this defensiveness when people say they want to "take a look at the data," but refuse to say how they interpret data. The natural defensiveness ruins what could be an excellent mode of operation for experimental design and statistics. Wouldn't it be nice if, in applied research, the decision makers would publicly state what data outcomes would cause them to make which decisions?

You have to *perceive* how your client's audience gets persuaded. It is important to know whether the audience likes or dislikes formal statistics. There are important audiences of clients who avoid formal statistical techniques because they can't understand them and don't trust statisticians. For such audiences, you need to keep your data presentation very simple, no more than means (medians) and scatter plots. For the extremely nonstatistical audiences, you almost have to describe results as an anecdote. Let us illustrate.

Number Phobes.   A client came to me to help design a study of the effectiveness of a camping program for crippled children. The private, nonprofit agency that runs the camp was running out of money and was ready to attempt a formal evaluation, using "studies" and "statistics." The agency had previously had plenty of money and was satisfied that most campers and their parents were happy with the camp. I worked with their agency and found that their staff is very warmhearted but extremely nonscientific and nonquantitative. I tried to talk to them in terms of what made them uneasy about the camp and why a study was needed. Everything they said about the camp was in terms of real anecodotes about real people. When I asked about rates of problem situations, they seemed confused and were able to say only whether some problem happened frequently or infrequently. They were uncomfortable with quantifying it, and I saw them persuade each other with a story like, "Remember two years ago when Kevin Lundberg . . . ?" All the staff could recall the Kevin Lundberg incident and were moved by the point made. When trying to describe something hypothetical, they would never use numbers. They would say something like, "Suppose we had a twelve-year-old retarded girl with cerebral palsy and . . . ." Then every one of the staff would listen and visualize such a case. They put everything in anecdote form. I gathered from some that they thought "statistics" were inhuman and irrelevant. They reminded me frequently that their campers are real people and not merely numbers.

I could see that no matter what the study results were, the staff would turn them into anecdotes. The outcomes were measured by answers to questionnaires. There were open-ended questions, with plenty of encouragement and room for comments. The study results were slightly positive, but essentially neutral. The way the staff dealt with that was to pick out the neutral comments from among the broad spectrum of parents' comments. Quoting a parent's comment seemed more real to the staff than numbers.

Number Freaks.   There are audiences at the other extreme who are real number freaks. Some of these can never get enough. They're dissatisfied with any study that "leaves something out." If they think something else could have been measured, they demand to know why it wasn't. This type of audience sometimes gives us a headache when they don't appreciate that long, tedious, mailed questionnaires have low response rates. We've gotten into debates with such audiences, defending clients against demands that questionnaire respondents should be conscientious. The urge to have every study milk all possible numbers and facts is strong in some audiences. These are tough audiences. They can never be totally satisfied, but it's good to know in advance if that's what your client is facing. Their demands are based on drive for thoroughness. At its worst, the drive is compulsive and indiscriminate.

Heterogeneous Audiences.   Other audiences want data presented in a crisp, clear form with no confusing extra appendages. They are annoyed with extraneous facts that distract them from main themes.

To better appreciate the great heterogeneity among your clients' audiences, simply note the discrepancies among statisticians in how they like to see data presented and what analysis should be used. There are nonparametric enthusiasts and neo-Bayesans and decision theorists who translate all statistical results into their own language. Even in statistics, it's not just what you say; it's how you say it and who's doing the listening. Government or industry clients have to communicate with scientists, administrators, and themselves. The rules governing persuasion in these three audiences are all distinctly different. Clients are very much individuals and very human. It's difficult for them to rise above what they want the data to say. Interpretation of one's own data is often as emotional as it is intellectual, and you see some clients clinging desperately to their own hoped-for interpretations. We recommend not arguing with stubborn clients about their interpretations of their data, but focusing your and your client's attention on communicating with administrative and scientific audiences.

It's more natural for statisticians to help clients communicate with scientific audiences. Scientists are used to technological advances, and many are receptive to more complicated statistical techniques. They tend more to respect statisticians and not to be so hostile to advanced statistical methods. Some of them are even more receptive to statistical methods that are new to them, liking to be on the frontier of new methodologies.

Convincing the Administrators

Administrators are a totally different breed. They are very pragmatic and honestly distrust statistical reasoning they don't understand. The reason is that they have to defend their discussions to people who distrust science and statistics. Let us illustrate.

In 1970, two administrators from my own university came to me asking for help in predicting enrollment for the university during the 1970s. The university is a landgrant institution and is always trying to get more money from the state legislature. The usual appeal for more money is based on the university's projected enrollment increases. In 1970, the legislature said it seriously distrusted the university's enrollment projections and told it to make better use of all its "high-powered statistics professors." The legislature was getting upset with the years of overestimating and wasn't able to follow the university's complicated formulas and use of fudge factors. They also expected statistics faculty to be more honest than administrators.

I saw the legislature as one audience that wanted very simple methods of projection used. They would distrust anything too fancy. The university officials were harder to figure out. They kept telling me three things: (1) They wanted me to be honest. (2) They wanted me to use sophisticated statistical techniques. (3) They said they wouldn't give me their fudge factor formulas because they might bias me.

I told them I thought the legislature probably wanted very primitive statistical methodology used so they wouldn't think they were being bamboozled. They told me not to worry about that but to go ahead and do what I thought statistically right. They also showed me a report written in 1960 by two statistics professors, giving several methods for student enrollment projections. I read it and said that it was very good and that I really couldn't do any better. They said they also presumed it was excellent but admitted they couldn't understand it. They were handed it in 1960 and tried to read it, but since then had simply let it collect dust. We agreed the legislature wouldn't understand it and that it would be bad to use it now and have to explain why they hadn't used it earlier.

I decided to give them something that sounded fancy but was also relevant. I used a Markov chain model and multiple regression, the phrases sounding impressive enough for anyone who wanted to be impressed. The model predicted that the university was heading away from the desired balance of graduates and undergraduates. This was useful information. It also predicted future enrollments, but with disturbingly wide confidence intervals.

The university officials were very conscientious and kept after me to reassure them I was "doing the right analysis." I said I was doing my best, but made two points: First, there are better and more famous statisticians who might given them more confidence and, second, in any real problem like this, there is no unique right analysis. I tried explaining the assumptions of the procedures I used, but they didn't know robustness; so they couldn't assess the importance of departing from the assumptions. I became annoyed (over a period of a few weeks) and said that they seemed very ambivalent about my projections. I offered to quit so that they could find a statistician in whom they would have more confidence. They assured me they didn't want another statistician, that I was "doing fine." I said there are only two ways a statistician can convince someone. Either the audience follows the logic of the statistical argument or trusts the statistician as an authority. There are no other ways I could make them comfortable, and I thought that neither one was working. I kept getting a double message; they reassured me when I threatened to resign, but otherwise kept checking up on me.

It turned out the next year that my predictions were not as good as the university's with their secret fudge factors. I wasn't surprised. I knew by the grapevine that they had several neat tricks to adjust for this and that and, in addition, were close to gossip sources as to which colleges were recruiting heavily and which had all the students it wanted. All the Markov chains and multiple regression in the world couldn't compensate for knowing the inside plans of the various colleges.

It was an extremely interesting consulting situation with several lessons in it. We focus here on the audience problem. There were two audiences: the clients and the legislature. The clients wanted me only because the legislature insisted on their using a statistics professor to work on the enrollment problem. They probably thought I was as good as the next one. The fact is that they didn't really believe in formal statistics, and there wasn't anything I could do to change their minds. There were not, and are not going to be, persuaded by formal statistics. They saw me as there for appearance's sake for the legislature. The legislature wanted me there because of their images of professors as more honest than the university administrators. What persuaded the legislature? Nothing, as far as we can tell. The funding battle continues.

CLIENTS' SUBCULTURES

An effective mind set in understanding how clients persuade their audiences is to think of them as belonging to a vocational subculture. They have to be able to communicate with others in that culture according to its customs. Engineers interact with and persuade each other differently than do business executives. For one engineer to be effective with another, she must show loyalty to the values of the engineering subculture.

To appreciate the demands a work group makes on its members, let us examine the values of statisticians. To please the statistical community and be accepted as a member in it, one must value carefulness and thoroughness of all thought processes and be against shallow research and superficiality. Statisticians are constantly apologizing to each other for cutting corners. They commonly state that they wanted to do a more thorough job than the one they did and blame lack of time or cooperation of clients for the imperfections. They want to reassure themselves and other statisticians.

Contrast the values of statisticians with the values of surgeons. Surgeons value thoroughness, but value good, bold decision making more. A surgeon who agonizes and frets over everything could never do any surgery. He'd never get the nerve to cut somebody open, knowing that the patient might die as a result. Surgeons will see someone who criticizes bold actions that are not preceded by extensive, careful plans as one who doesn't understand surgery.

The difference between the *values* of statistics and surgery explains much of the difficulty statisticians and surgeons have with each other. Statisticians think surgeons are too careless in their research, and surgeons think statisticians are too picky. They tend to avoid and gripe about each other. A statistician who is going to be effective helping one surgeon persuade other surgeons is well advised to understand their values. Surgeons live in a chaotic (by statisticians' standards) world of interuptions, bold decisions, and on-the-spot compromise. They typically have much missing data due to the realities of their practices and ethical constraints. They are looking for statistical analyses that are classical and simple because they don't trust the fancy and complicated. They will use boldly whatever tools you give them and rely heavily on a traditional and well-accepted procedure.

Surgeons, like other physicians, have a different view of what constitutes statistical correctness. It is based on the method by which a surgical procedure becomes accepted. Sometimes a surgeon will claim that a technique works only when he uses it, arguing that only he knows how to do it right. This can be true, because surgical skill is a very important ingredient, and some surgeons are almost uniquely talented. The other method of proof, clearly less egocentric, is that a technique works no matter which surgeon uses it and no matter which city it is used in. This makes great sense, but it has an interesting corollary. Surgeons may think a statistical procedure is legitimate because it has been shown to work in a variety of settings over a long time by a wide variety of statistical practitioners. The idea of introducing a new technique because it "looks good on paper" (we call it a mathematical proof) doesn't give them confidence. They're used to seeing many ideas that sound good or work in the artificial setting of a laboratory but just don't work out in practice. In general, they're very suspicious of untried theories. They're not keen on your thinking up a new statistical analysis to use on their data. They can't defend a new statistical procedure to their colleagues. With surgeons, then, use the tried and true statistical techniques if at all possible.

In contrast to surgeons, economists are much more in the market for new statistical techniques and clever new ways of thinking. Economists have a very difficult time with their public image. Everyone gives them a hard time because economists of differing philosophies make widely discrepant predictions. Economists can't get together and speak in one voice. There will always be economists, however, because the demand for economic predictions will always exist. Because of the demand for fresh ideas in economics, the field is more open to new mathematical methodology. With economists, you have a more receptive audience for the new, complicated statistical technique.

By far the best technique for getting to know a client's subculture is to spend time with it. Get to know some people in it and know them professionally as well as you can. It also helps greatly to know them personally as well as how they think and what they value. It's invaluable to know how they argue with each other and what are the techniques they use to win arguments. Get a sense of how much they appeal to authority (that is, leaders of the field) and how cautious are they in trying new ideas. The cautious fields need overwhelming evidence before making any changes. Other fields are kind of "loose," with rapid changes made on the basis of a few shreds of evidence. Another fact to learn is how much the field believes in research and statistics and how much statistical sophistication people in it can stand. Learn their favorite statistical techniques and how much they believe in them.

SUMMARY

• Find out who the client's audiences are and their attitudes toward statistics. Find out how they persuade each other and try to communicate with them in their manner as much as you can.

• Some clients have to report their results to audiences that distrust all statisticians and formal statistical procedures. For these audiences, only graphs and tables are persuasive.

• Graphs and tables are effective for every audience.

CHAPTER 7

Business Aspects of Consulting

We think we deal with clients fairly. We carry out our part of the bargain and hope they will carry out theirs. Unfortunately, sometimes our definitions of "fair" differ. I worked on a project for six months, assuming that the client and I were co-authors. It became clear, however, that my payoff at the end of the effort would be a footnote rather than co-authorship of the report. Later, to my even greater chagrin, I discovered I would also have minimal control over how my statistical analyses would be used. Working on these misunderstandings and resolving them as well as we could after the work had been done wasted much time, caused bitterness in both me and the client, and undercut the quality of the science that was done on that project. We've both had more than one case like this. This experience has motivated us to move from "hope" that our clients will carry out their part of the bargain to negotiating our working relationship.

NEGOTIATIONS

Negotiation is essential in all consultations. You and your client have several things to negotiate if the consultation is going to be successful. Although the list of questions to consider depends on you, your job, your goals, and comparable characteristics of your client, we list some of the most common ones to consider.

1. What tasks are to be done?
2. Who will do them? Who has what responsibilities?
3. How will you resolve authorship of the report? Or, in an industrial setting, who will get what credit for what parts of the work?
4. How much time is available for the project?
5. How much money will this project cost?
6. Will you be paid a fee for your services? How much? When? How?
7. Who will decide when the work is done?
8. Who will do the quality control of the variables to be measured?
9. What type of relationship will you have with this client?
10. Are there other parties involved in this consultation who are not present today? What are their roles?
11. Who has to agree on the final report? Who will write it? How will agreements be reached? Will it be a consensus procedure or will "majority rule" be followed?
12. How will the statistical work you do be presented? How will your report be used? What control will you have over this?
13. Will you prepare a written report of your activities?

14. What is your client's position in the client organization? What is expected of him or her?

15. What is the organizational chart for the project, relating the client, his or her boss, the funding agency, and perhaps the regulatory agency?

16. Can you remain neutral on this case if it involves a legal issue that may end up in court?

Timing

You won't discuss all these issues in the first session with your client; some will not become relevant until later. If you are busy, you may want to avoid these topics. However, be careful of this inclination; it can easily become penny-wise and pound-foolish, as was the case in the story we just told. It is possible to discuss some nitty-gritty issues and still keep the interaction with your client on a friendly level. You need not be argumentative to discuss them. In fact, the relationship will probably be healthier in the long run if you are up front and deal with some of these issues early in the relationship because some are appropriate to resolve in the first session. These issues are always easiest to deal with at the beginning of the relationship, before anyone has invested any effort in the project. Not all these questions need to be resolved before you start on a project with a client. As you become more experienced, you will develop a better idea as to which should be resolved earlier in a relationship and which you are willing to make assumptions about or resolve later. Let the client know what assumptions you make, but do it in a helpful rather than a defensive-legalistic manner.

Sensitive Issues

Some of these issues are difficult to discuss with the client. Most of us dread confrontations and are afraid of a scene that might end in a hostile relationship. This fear can get in the way of good science in that many of these questions have to be resolved if the project is going to be done well. It is understandable if you find it difficult to discuss some of these matters. We do. It is worthwhile in the long run to discuss them, however. Negotiation skill helps your consultations be more successful and more efficient. The reason to negotiate these issues is that unrealistic expectations commonly exist between consultant and client. Your client, for example, may expect you to be a research assistant, statistical adviser, collaborator, keypunch operator, and computer programmer. You may erroneously expect your clients to be perfectly willing to commit themselves to several consulting sessions, to read methodological articles relating to how to use statistics in their problem, or to allow you to use their data set as an example in a research article you are preparing. You and your clients may have quite different expectations regarding the subsequent use of their data. Some clients will not allow anyone else to use any of their data. There are even clients who won't let anyone outside their small circle of research colleagues *see* their data.

Unequal Power

Power and status differences between you and your clients make it uncomfortable to discuss expectations with the client. You may be new with the company; whereas your client is a respected scientist who has been there twenty years. Alternatively, you may be the eminent statistical consultant in the group and the client, the new chemist in the company. If we are to believe sociologists and social psychologists, no amount of open discussion will completely eliminate the effects of these status differences. It will help you to deal with the issue of power and status if you have a clear picture of your job responsibilities and what sorts of tasks your consulting group does. These are issues to resolve *before* you encounter a client who triggers these concerns. We urge you to discuss these status issues with your colleagues and supervisors.

We find that the discussion or negotiation part of a consulting session can almost always be done in a friendly manner. In a healthy relationship, firmness does not ruin friendliness. A relationship is healthier if both parties are kind, firm, and fair to each other. It helps *enormously* if they understand and emphathize with each other. Your clients particularly want to be reassured that you will not abandon them. They want to know that you are committed to the goal of making the study work. Any reticence on your part will be detected.

Key Issues in Agreements

The results of your negotiations may be presented in just a verbal agreement on specific matters. They may also be presented in a more formal way, ranging from a memo addressed to all parties present at the consulting session to a written legal contract detailing all aspects of the relationship. It is often a good idea to send out a memo summarizing who is going to do what. We suggest a formal contract if it is a private consultation with you being paid directly.

There are many questions to be answered in a negotiation, whether it be recorded verbally or in writing. For example, as you are to begin to work with a client on the analysis of data he has spent the last three years gathering, it is time to clarify your and your client's assumptions about the data set. Is it in good shape? Are you going to check it? Is he going to pay you to do this? How long will that take? Who is going to clear up problems in the data set? Are your time estimates based on the assumption that the data set as it is currently stored in the computer is correct? If so, you had better clarify that. In one case where I did not do this, the data set in the computer had major errors in it, contrary to my assumptions, and I almost lost $5,000. The contract did not make it clear what had been assumed about the quality of the data. We always make sure we cover three key issues in negotiations with clients.

Payment and Terms. What fee should you charge and when will you be paid? Most statistical consultants tend to sell their services too cheaply. To estimate what professionals in your locality charge, talk to individuals in other professions to learn their fee schedules. One method is to call a friend who is a lawyer and ask how much dentists or doctors or engineers who are called as expert witnesses on legal cases charge for their services. This may be an eye-opener. You are worth a professional fee for your services. You spent many years working to achieve the competencies that you have.

When will you be paid? Don't leave the total payment to the end of the project. Bills tend to mount up and look larger than the client thought they would. Furthermore, weekly or monthly payment provides an automatic monitoring of the statistical consulting cost in the project. It enables you and the client to catch overruns before they have gotten too large. Negotiating this topic is too easily neglected when time is short. Very often, everyone will think in the heat of the battle that the fees have been taken care of, only to discover later that far more consulting time than the client had expected has been required to resolve the crisis.

I was once involved in a crisis consulting case in which the client and the consulting firm assumed that the fee had been set. Unfortunately, the consulting bill was approximately twice what the client had anticipated. The bill shocked the client, and we spent many hours of negotiation working out a compromise billing. The firm lost several thousands of dollars of billable services in the process of compromising and I lost $1,500.

I recall another crisis case in which an eminent lawyer assured me that when the crisis was over, my services to the state would be reimbursed at a fair professional rate. Unfortunately, when the crisis was over, the lawyer's attention turned to her next case. She had little recollection of how hard I had worked, how many nights I had stayed up, or what results I had obtained under the time pressure of the crisis. I never did recoup the substantial fees I should have been paid. In part, this was due to timidity on my part; I was reluctant to force the issue. The major reason for not collecting for my services was that I had done a poor job of negotiating at the beginning of that crisis project. We had no formal agreement on how the fees would be handled.

I did not follow up on the case and remind the lawyer of her assurances. I waited for her to take care of me as she "should have" but didn't. Clients are busy and even without malicious intent won't worry about your interests. They have other things to do. If you are like me, you feel uncomfortable negotiating a contract with a client. However, the comfort experienced in not negotiating a contract is usually short-lived. The small amount of time and discomfort spent on negotiating simple verbal contracts even in crisis cases where time is short is well worth it. The alternative is that you may end up being totally altruistic with your time and contributing it to the client with no fee paid.

Time Estimates.   On what assumptions are your time estimates based? Have you made them all explicit? How have you estimated the time required to complete this project? We frequently break the task up into small components and estimate the time required to do a particular component. We also spend an hour or two or a day or two on the project, depending on its magnitude, before giving a final estimate as to the time required to complete it. During this time, we look at the computer data files, if they have already been constructed, checking a random sample of the computer data against the data from the raw data sheets. We also look at the raw data and talk to others who have worked in the field in order to identify potential pitfalls. When this estimate has been constructed, we multiply by two or three in order to get a reasonably safe estimate of the time that will actually be required to wrap up the project. In your estimation process, plan to handle the *additional* requests for statistical help that the client will almost assuredly make.

Credit.   How will you resolve issues relating to authorship, the use of your work and reports, and credit for what was done? This can be very sensitive. Everybody likes to be acknowledged and rewarded for their work, though some investigators are uneasy about sharing authorship or credit. Deming (1965) makes very firm statements as to how his materials can be used and how they will be related to the final report. He suggests that you present a report on your work and insist on it appearing in the final report, with you having the right to see other materials that are presented with yours. He also retains the right to compose a minority report if he disagrees with the project report. Although you may not choose to negotiate such an explicit agreement, it is desirable to agree on how your report will be used and particularly how it will relate to the final project report. Do not assume that just because you have done statistical work and presented it in a way that you consider to be clear the client will use it the way you want or come up with valid conclusions based on what you have done.

TIME MANAGEMENT

It is essential that the effective statistician be good at managing time. This involves controlling time and predicting how long things take. Many statisticians are very good technically but cannot handle the time aspects of a consulting practice. One reason some statisticians can't manage time is that as people they can't manage time. Time management has little to do with intelligence or mathematical statistical ability. It's simply a separate skill. Another reason some statisticians are bad at time management is their perfectionism. They are so anxious to do a good, thorough job on each project that they have long time overruns. Such statisticians are best suited for handling very few clients. It you are perfectionistic and uncomfortable with conflicts between time binds and work quality, you may need to take clients sequentially (that is, don't take the next client until this one is done). That system works well for statisticians who have clients willing to wait for them, no matter how long it takes. Perfectionist statisticians need clients who are not in a rush and can allow them all the time they want. This arrangement is sometimes workable in a university, with the statistician being a tenured professor not needing (for salary increases or promotion) any client's approval.

Deadlines

Once the statistician is working outside the academic world, however, the problems of time management are great. Most clients have deadlines, and when clients have deadlines, consultants have deadlines. Many clients' deadlines are inflexible. In principle, having a number of clients with firm deadlines is simply a mathematics problem. In practice, it is more or less overwhelming. Before facing the time problems of having several clients, let's see what they are with only one ordinary client who has his own deadline.

Client Ignorance. The most basic reason for time problems with a client with a deadline is that the client doesn't know how long statistical things take. Some clients will come to you with so little time allowed for statistical work that you can't do anything at all. Recently, somebody stood impatiently in my open doorway while I was talking to someone else. I was trying to finish the conversation I was in, but the guy in the doorway interrupted me in mid-sentence and asked if he could talk to me for a minute. I said that I would talk to him after I finished my conversation, which should be over within ten minutes. He said he couldn't wait ten minutes, and what he wanted would just take a second. Getting annoyed, but trying to show only a little of it, I asked him what it was. He said he had a question about statistics. I said, "I've never been able to answer a statistics question in a second before." He pressed again, saying he was in a great hurry. I gave a slightly exasperated sigh, and asked a junior colleague if she had time to talk to a client. She agreed to do so.

This took place at 4 P.M. on a Friday. The client had wanted me to arrange for him, before 5 P.M., to get some cards punched from coding sheets and regression lines calculated. He was catching a plane on Sunday to give a talk on Monday and needed his data analyzed for the talk. My colleague told him, trying not to show irritation, that it was impossible for us to do this on short notice, but said the client could do a very minimal analysis by connecting the two extreme points of each data set, forming a line by a method that throws away much of the data. He could get some blank transparencies before 5 P.M. and plot the lines by himself on Saturday. He acted very grateful, apologized for being so ignorant of how much he had asked for, and went away. We never saw or heard from him again. This was near the ultimate in quick-and-dirty consultations, only the phone call consultations being quicker and dirtier. The story brings up many issues, such as what should we have done differently, technically. Should I have angrily dismissed him while scolding him for being so inconsiderate? The point here is that his reason for the impossible request was genuine ignorance.

Client Arrogance.   Another form of client ignorance is their not allowing you enough time to work on their problems, expecting you to drop your other commitments and work for them full time. This reason for the client's poor planning of your time has a different psychological effect on you. It is insulting for clients to assume that you don't have any other commitments or that those you do have are obviously less important than your commitment to them. Clients who assume you will drop all other work and devote full time to their problem can make you angry enough to think more about getting back at them than solving their statistics problem. The implication, if you let it get to you, is that they think their work is more important than the work of your other clients, and they assume this without finding out about your other clients' work. Does this happen to you? It happens to us often enough.

Client Inadequacies.   The third reason for time problems with clients with deadlines is different from ignorance of how long statistical work takes and different from arrogance. Some of them say, when I plead crowded schedule, that *their* work is *really important*.

There are clients who know how long statistical work takes and realize that I have other clients whose work is equally important, but who are simply terrible at managing even their own time. I've been working with one client for over two years whose personal and professional life is a time disaster. I've gone over the point with her again and again, saying that no statistician could do well with the short time she allows. I remind her that last time I had to do a sad rescue attempt at analysis because she didn't come to me with the design problem. She and I have gone through this a number of times. I *think* she would like to bring me the design problems, but forgets. Her time management problem is that to have the design discussion with me, she'd have to get me and some lab technicians together. First, she'd have to find them. Then, she'd have to dovetail her schedule, theirs, and mine. It doesn't work for me to talk directly to her lab techs because they see her as their boss and, for their job security, do what she says. This is a problem because she changes her mind frequently on the design. She also can't understand that sample size determination depends on variability and so forth. Are you wondering whether she's a good scientist? I don't think she is. Do you wonder why I don't get rid of her as a client? The reason is her political position relative to mine. This reason may be difficult for some readers to accept, but it is real, and this book is about the realities of consultation. I do think this client means well. We'll talk later about dealing with those who don't.

Your Associates.   We now see there are at least three reasons for clients with deadlines causing consulting time problems, but clients are but one source of difficulty. The people you depend on to get part of the work done (those who do keypunching, coding, graphing, and programming, if you are not doing them yourself) are a vital part of the statistics process, but having these assistants and associates requires that you be very aware of *their* schedules.

Some statisticians refuse to be responsible for the data-processing aspects of statistics and make it the client's problem to arrange for those services. This relieves them of an enormous administrative burden and hands it right over to the client. If it is the client's *first* time at being a client, he may think it very reasonable that he arrange for data processing. If it's his *second* time, however, he'll be grateful if you'll arrange the contracts and scheduling of those services. It can be a big scheduling headache, which is why neither of you wants to do it. It complicates your life greatly, but we recommend it for the consultant who wants happy clients. Refusing to do it gives the same appearance as a doctor who says you need X-rays and lab tests, then says it's up to you to find a place that will do them.

If you take on responsibility for arranging for all auxiliary statistical services, you have time problems. When the statistical work isn't done on time because a coder got sick, the client holds you responsible, and you are. There are some good excuses, of course, and many understanding clients in this world, but it better not happen too often. Your skill at managing time is worth its weight in gold in client satisfaction.

Good Techniques and Goodwill

We are keenly aware that telling you how good it is for you to manage time doesn't make it easy to do. It is a skill not taught in school. It involves prediction of how long all kinds of things take and building in a time cushion. If other people do the coding and keypunching, it requires your knowing them well and how fast they work. You also need to know their schedules. What you really need is their goodwill so that you can cash in a few chips and get them to bail you out of an emergency. You better not have too many emergencies, unless you have power over them. Even if you do have power over them, they'll see you as disorganized and inconsiderate if your emergency rate is too high. Keeping several projects going in a variety of stages of development, with some of your clients being bad time managers themselves, can really keep you hopping. It gets chaotic. But in-the-trenches consultants have to take clients whether or not they like them and their problems. They have to do something with them; they can't evict them all. One principle is crucial for avoiding time binds: Whenever you can, use techniques and people and systems you're familiar with. Time chaos is just around the corner when you try a new technique that is over your head.

I remember one big study that was time chaos all by itself. I didn't need anything else for pressure and tension. There was a mountain of data, collected on thousands of subjects with thousands of observations per subject. There were about fifteen investigators on the research project who wanted this or that calculated, printed out, and sent to them for their perusal. The data files were in fairly bad shape. The person who had the tapes in a distant city dragged his heels in getting us the tapes. Badly collected and irrelevant variables had to be tossed. The fifteen people who wanted results were impatient with me because I was telling the programmer which analyses to do first. That whole project was wild. Frankly, I felt a sense of accomplishment just getting it done on time without running out of money. As far as I know, there aren't any big mistakes in it. To meet that project deadline, I had to use *very* familiar techniques, systems, and people, although there was considerable pressure from some of the fifteen to use more exotic statistical techniques. Scientifically, they were right. Practically, I can defend my shortcuts. It sure needed shortcuts. One co-investigator wanted all the correlations printed out so he could look at them. "Look at them?" I said. "How? There are over twelve million correlations." The ensuing debate was lively but led to a friendly resolution. (Note that the statistician confronted the co-investigator, who wanted all the correlations printed. This "lively" discussion did cause discomfort for both the statistician and the co-investigator. However, they worked through this short-term discomfort to a resolution of the problem.) This experience, along with a few dozen others, illustrates a key principle: *It doesn't matter how good it is if it's not done on time.*

Your Consultation Style

The hard question of time management is how conservative to be. Should you be cautious in order to make sure you meet every deadline of each client? We statisticians know from queuing theory that such a strategy will create considerable idle time for us. Time conservatism is a key issue in deciding how many clients to handle at once. Statisticians who can't stand time overruns will need to handle fewer clients. Statisticians in constant chaos will have several clients breathing down their neck, nagging them to get moving on their projects. Some statisticians, just like people in general, get so used to being in chaos that it seems like the natural state; when their life gets a little uncluttered, they make some more commitments and thus increase their tension level again. What philosophy should you adopt? There is no one answer. You already have your own temperament and a natural pace at which you live your life. Your natural pace is very difficult to change. We do want to point out a serious drawback to the overcautious extreme, however. Being so cautious that you never have a time overrun sounds superficially admirable but implies you're not handling all the clients you can.

Quality or Quantity. The time allocation question brings up the dilemma of whether to help a few clients thoroughly, letting the others you don't have time for do their work without statistical help, or to help all of them some. You can argue that clients you don't have time for aren't your responsibility, but the argument is not airtight. It can be argued that if you do a few clients perfectly, you will develop the reputation of a hard-to-get master. Clients who can't get even an appointment with you to bounce off some ideas may be impressed that you're a highly sought after statistician, but may feel snubbed if you can't give them at least a quick hearing.

We have a firm recommendation. If somebody wants to see you or just wants to see a statistician, don't cut him or her off short. Grant or get a colleague to grant at least one brief hearing. At least find out who the client is, what the project is, and what he or she wants from a statistician. You don't have to promise to do anything, but you have a chance to explain why you are full up and either refer the client to another statistician or explain why you can't. There is great political benefit to giving all clients some sort of a hearing, even if it's a brief phone call, and this policy can be defended on scientific grounds. Don't be worried that each person you talk to will become your client and thus expand your client load beyond your time management ability. It's just a matter of making clear that the person is not yet a client, but that you have concern for all your potential clients. In a brief interview, you can find out if the person has big statistical needs, small statistical needs, or no statistical needs at all. You can find out about money and time limitations. It's like a military medical triage, separating the wounded into three classes when there's a shortage of medical help: (1) Can't use help (going to die no matter what you do). (2) Doesn't need help (will get well no matter what you do). (3) Will make good use of help. If your style is to handle a few clients well, meeting all their deadlines, the policy of giving at least one hearing to everyone who appears at the door gives you a much friendlier image.

Reigning Chaos. Let's consider the other extreme of style, with too many clients and frequent missed deadlines. Just putting this style down on paper makes it seem bad. It's foreign to the temperament of most statisticians; they are instinctively in favor of keeping the world tight and tidy. Yet there are statisticians who are intellectually in favor of the organized life, doing careful, thorough statistical jobs, but because of their temperament, using a time-chaotic consulting style. Let's discuss its root causes, consequences, and techniques for changing it.

Statisticians whose time style is chaotic may use it for one or more of the following reasons. First, they may simply be bad at estimating how long things take to do and live in the hope that from now on things will go better and they will eventually get more organized. This type of person often has a bad memory, forgetting how long things take. They make new commitments because they forget the ones they've already made. Statisticians who sincerely want to correct this pattern are advised to get a friend or secretary who is good at time management and very firm to keep reminding them how busy they are. These statisticians should check every new commitment for reasonableness with the friend (secretary). Truly wanting to change is crucial. If not sincere, these statisticians keep laying all the burden of being the villain on the reminding person. It then degenerates into a game, with the reminding person resentful that he or she can't get the cooperation of the forgetful person.

Another reason for the statistician using a chaotic style is a strong workaholic drive. Some statisticians, like some people in general, seek a very high level of activity. To the observer, it looks like the hyperactive person is always running. This workaholic behavior wins many accolades from society and is difficult to change without a heart attack. Some workaholics accomplish a great deal, but others put in huge amounts of time and energy inefficiently because of chronic fatigue and burnout. The problem workaholics have with client deadlines is an overcommitment for the purpose of guaranteeing that they keep busy. They can't stand idle time or lack of pressure because idleness makes them more anxious than heavy work loads. A statistician of this nature tends to take on too many clients to guarantee busyness. We know of no solutions to the time problems of the disorganized workaholic. Solution to the problems requires a basic change in life orientation. The compulsive working often serves some function for the person and may be an unbreakable habit.

Third, statisticians whose basic nature is to please others often get into time troubles through saying yes to too many clients in order not to hurt their feelings. This type of statistician is destined always to be apologizing to clients for not meeting deadlines. Clients like these statisticians personally, but soon give up on their ability to get organized. They can say no only when their schedule is bursting at the seams, thus guaranteeing time chaos and/or an ulcer. The only way out for them is to have someone else (a supervisor, say) say no for them. The supervisor should say to the client, "Frank would like to take you on as a client, but I've already overassigned him and decided to reduce his work load. He's getting burned out and he's too valuable to be wasted." When the potential client goes to Frank to see if he can't squeeze him in, Frank can pass the blame by saying, "I'd really like to, but my supervisor is getting upset with my overcommitment."

MONEY MANAGEMENT

It's been said that time is money. The statement has enough inherent truth to keep it alive as a business maxim. There is an obvious connection, but they require separate managing skills.

Price Estimation

Although one may view doing statistics anywhere on the moral spectrum from a business to a profession to a noble calling, clients want to be treated in a more or less "businesslike" manner. Just as they want to know how long the statistical work will take, they want to know how much it will cost. Perhaps you and your clients work for the same company or government agency without a cross-charge system. In that situation, the negotiations involve time only. If money is not involved, the queue discipline is very different. The clients who become dependent on you will demand as much of your time and attention as you will give them because it doesn't cost them or their unit any money. Without the practical boundary of money, how much time you spend working on various clients' problems depends on their political power, how much you like them personally, how valuable you think their work is, how clear their problem is, and such. One of the frustrations of statistical consultation is the realization that almost every client's problem can consume infinite time and money by pursuing tangents and exploring assumptions through Monte Carlo studies. Thus, without the limitation of money, limits must be set by other criteria. Often these limits are set unconsciously rather than consciously.

Let's consider the case in which the client, directly or by third party, pays money for statistical work. Her question is, "How much will it cost?" You say to yourself, "How much will *what* cost?" Her question is like asking how much groceries cost, or hospital stays cost. You know the answer depends on many things. As you start to explain the wide spectrum of possible costs, you see you're not getting anywhere. After listening for awhile, she says she just wants her data analyzed (experiment designed) and wants you to give her a cost estimate. Try as you will to explain that she can buy a minimal analysis or a maximal analysis, and that either end of the spectrum is scientifically defensible, you realize she can't make the decision; she just wants it done right. Client expectations of the money cost of statistics covers the waterfront. I've had people come to me with fifty observations in a t-test type of problem ready to spend $200 and others come in with $1,000 worth of work and be shocked that the bill will exceed $100. Some first-time clients think there is no charge at all, that they are doing me a favor to *let* me do something with their data because they assume statisticians are sexually aroused by fondling numbers.

A good way to start on price estimation is to find out how much data was, or will be, collected and in what form. This may be a logical circle if you are designing the study because *you* will help decide how much data to collect, and in what form. The cost of data storage and retrieval (including coding, keypunching, and programming) is easier to estimate than the cost of analysis if the client is the type to analyze and reanalyze the data.

To estimate the costs of data collection and storage, there is no substitute for talking to the workers who collect and store. Cost estimation for storage is an essential skill. Find and get to know people who are good at it and give straight answers. Such people are invaluable to you. Estimating the cost of keypunching from good coding sheets is easy, but estimating coding costs is hard. Estimating the cost of setting up data files on computers takes much computer experience. Get to know people who are able and willing to make estimates for you. If you can't pay them financially for the estimation, make sure they feel rewarded by your appreciation or whatever else you can do for them. Remember, we strongly advise against making the client work out the negotiations for data storage unless he or she definitely wants to. It *can* work out if the client contracts for your services and contracts separately for computer services, but it is usually a big headache for the average client.

Money Limitations

A key impact of money limitations on statistical work is that it forces hard choices on the statistician. It obviously makes the ideal, comprehensive search for the ultimate truth unaffordable. Money limitations, just like time limitations, demand that the statistician compromise. The primary frustration for the statistician is the denial of the basic drive to be *thorough.* Statisticians are selected and trained for thoroughness. They are reminded by statistical speakers and journals that thoroughness is a high virtue. Shortcuts are seen as sins, forgiven only for pressing external limitations. Statisticians typically justify their shortcuts by citing time limitations. Statisticians who say publicly what they actually did in a real situation almost always say that they would have been more thorough (for example, checking assumptions or using alternate analyses) if there had been more time. They less often mention the shortage of money.

One day a client came in with a marketing problem for hospital clinics. He was carrying four computer tapes containing data on 180,000 patients for almost 600,000 outpatient visits. He had essentially complete data on each patient's age, sex, type of payment, and place of residence. He had the hospital costs they incurred and wanted to find out which groups are the biggest spenders on hospital services. That is, he wanted to know to which groups the hospital should appeal for business. (You are invited to notice how you *feel* about this client's goals. Do they violate your image of what a hospital should be? Do they alter your desire to help him? Note the impact of these nonstatistical issues on you.)

There were technique decisions I had to make. This client was actually low on the totem pole of his study. He had two bosses, one of whom is not sophisticated quantitatively, but controls the money. The other knows quite a bit about statistics and wanted him to do some fairly complicated maneuvers. The former wanted something she could understand.

With as much data as he had, just the retrieval costs of running through the tapes would be high. I asked him how much money he had to spend, saying that I needed to know how big a random sample to take off the tapes. He said money was not a problem; he had a grant for the computer. I asked him how much the grant was for. He said, "A hundred and fifty dollars, but I can get more." He didn't know how much more. "Maybe $50 more," he said. I asked him how much he could get totally. He wouldn't say. Then I said, "Are we talking a couple of thousand?" (I assessed that this client had a very high ego strength and that pushing him on this would not cause him to withhold information or otherwise fail to cooperate.) He said, "Two thousand is really pushing it." I countered with, "How about a thousand? Would that cause you any trouble? I sure don't want to get you in trouble with Joan!" I know Joan, the boss with the money. She is very pragmatic and would not trust my client's judgment if he spent too much on scientific adventures.

He said, "One thousand would be a lot better, but I'm not sure. I think I'd be pushing it with $1,000." Then I said, "Five hundred?" His face relaxed and he said, "There's no problem with $500." I replied, "Good. I'll talk to some computer experts and see what we can do for $500. I'm really at a loss right now on how big a sample we can get off the tape. I know Joan will want some rough descriptive figures, but you say that Vern (the other boss) is asking for discriminant analysis on the two extremes of costs. Do you suppose Vern wants to make the analysis decisions?" He said he didn't know what role Vern wants to play. Then I said, "Well, I can talk to Vern when I'm trying to see what we can do for $500."

I really didn't know how much it would cost just to access the data on those tapes. The problem was to choose a small enough sample from which to make another tape for analyses. It's *very easy* to use up $500, counting my time, programmers, and junior statistician's time.

You may wonder, if the money was so limited, if an adequate analysis could be done. Sometimes that is the case, but not often. There's usually a very broad spectrum of plausible analyses, requiring wide ranges of time and money. A statistician can almost always do *some analysis*, but almost never do a *complete* analysis. Most practicing statisticians live in this broad, ill-defined arena.

IDENTIFYING THE REAL CLIENT

To increase your effectiveness, learn the organization chart for the project. The organization chart will explain much of what the client does, who his or her bosses are, who is formally in charge of this project, who makes the major decisions, who is the funding agency, and which regulatory agency monitors the work. Another view of the chart is obtained by talking to individuals in the company other than the client about the problem. (You may even find that there are powerful people within the company who do not want the problem solved.)

Dealing with "Messengers"

Recently, two people came to see me about a problem they were having with a large survey of several institutions. The data had already been collected. The clients said they had contracted with a nationally prestigious survey firm, who had set up the sampling design. The survey firm representative had given weights to adjust the estimates, but the clients couldn't figure out how to use the weights. They had asked the survey firm representative for clarification, but the latter was impatient with them, giving them a written example of how to use the weights. The clients couldn't follow the example and were too intimidated to ask for further help. Somebody referred them to me.

I also had a hard time understanding the weighting scheme, and after understanding it, I disagreed with it. After some discussion, I said I could adopt any one of three strategies: (1) Show them how to use the weights they were instructed to use. (2) Because there was so much missing data, do a simple, unweighted estimation. (3) Try to figure out a better weighting scheme.

The main point of the example is that they slowly, in an embarrassed manner, revealed that they had little deciding authority. They had a supervisor who had the power to decide what philosophy of analysis to adopt. They guessed that he would prefer my suggestion for unweighted estimates because it sounded simpler and would cost less. They went away and called back in two days, saying that it had been decided to use the weights the survey consultant had recommended. I tried to ask them gently if their supervisor had changed his mind, but they wouldn't tell me who had made the decision. They thanked me for my help and said they would possibly contact me later. After polite conversation, I asked them where to send the bill. "Bill?" the leader said. "I had no idea you were charging for your services!" I reminded her that she had said early on that money was no problem and that my assistant had worked about $100 worth in assessing the problem. I admitted that I hadn't specifically mentioned billing them, but that it was customary. The client sounded miffed, but would try to find a way to pay if it was absolutely necessary. I said that it wasn't absolutely necessary and that I was perhaps at fault for not making it clear at the beginning, after she had said that there was plenty of money for statistical help. That's where it ended.

What went wrong? The money loss was small enough and admittedly I hadn't been clear. I usually am direct at the outset about charges. The question was who had the power to decide. At first I thought it was their boss, but their switch from "He'll surely go for the simpler analysis" to using the weights the survey consultant had recommended confused me. Why their defensive refusal to tell me who made the decision? They definitely did not want me to talk to their boss. I thought I hadn't turned them off personally, but will never know. It was apparent they didn't want me to know the authority structure of the study.

I often find I am talking to a client who is essentially a messenger and has no authority to make decisions. This is far from ideal. Finding out who has authority to decide is important in statistical consultation, but it isn't always easy. It helps to know it because you then know with whom you're trying to communicate. It's preferable not to try to do it through a messenger disguised as a client. Statistical communication is hard enough without going through a messenger. One of the big questions is, "Is the person you're talking to the real client?"

It's easy to forget to ask this question. Young veterinarians who go into small-animal practice (treating pets) soon learn to appreciate that their business depends not on treating pets, but owners of pets. It doesn't matter how happy their pets are. It matters how happy their *clients* (pet owners) are.

Identifying the Decision Maker

As important as it is to find out the organization chart of a study, it isn't always easy. The difficulty is in the distinction between formal and informal authority. In other words, who's really the decision maker?

The subtlety of identifying the decision maker is illustrated by the story of Little Red Riding Hood (LRRH). As you recall, LRRH found herself in the woods going to her grandmother's house. She ran into much trouble with a wolf, who scared her to death. She had to be rescued by a woodsman. Her grandmother was eaten by the wolf, and the woodsman killed the wolf. Who was responsible for all that carnage? How about LRRH's parent(s)? Weren't they the ones who left their daughter running around those woods and left the grandmother alone in a shack?

You may be more frustrated if you find out who has what decision power in a consultation, but you're likely to be more effective. The frustration occurs when you find you can't talk directly to the decider. Sometimes it is the decider who doesn't want to talk to you, for fear of looking foolish in front of a statistician. Other times, it is the messenger who wants to keep you and the decider apart. This strategy gives the messenger much power. Whether or not you like the reasons, they are often unchangeable. I once asked a messenger to let me talk to the decider and was told that I would be sued if I even attempted it. This situation is one of many statisticians face that can seriously frustrate them. Statisticians resent the problems of science caused by human nature. They are in trouble if they are not willing to face this reality, as opposed to complaining about it. There are problems in science caused by human nature.

A physician client, Dr. Baxter, brought some data on surgical patients to a statistical consultant, Tom. Dr. Baxter seemed mentally sharp and understood the logic of what she wanted, but wanted to turn it over to Tom to "get it done." She thought there wasn't much going on in her data but didn't want to say so to her peers until a statistician looked it over for possible gems. She supposed Tom would do that. There was much missing data because many patients wouldn't come back for follow-up tests if they felt well. Tom decided that the first step was to get the data on punch cards and asked Dr. Baxter about time and money constraints. Her answer was discouraging. Time was short, and she couldn't get much money. Tom suggested that one of Dr. Baxter's subordinates, a nurse, do the coding because there were medical interpretations to be made that required medical expertise. Dr. Baxter said that was a good idea and that her nurse assistant, Linda, had plenty of time and could do it easily.

Dr. Baxter sent Linda to meet with Tom for him to explain the coding to her. Linda had a very different perception of her time than Dr. Baxter did, however. She complained that Dr. Baxter had her buried in work, and her doing the coding to meet this deadline would simply cause her to get further behind on her other work. Linda told Tom that Dr. Baxter is always doing this to her. She keeps piling on work and seems to forget how much she's already assigned her. Linda admits that she's not very assertive and that the very assertive Dr. Baxter either doesn't get her subtle complaints about her work load or else doesn't care. Tom admitted to himself that Linda is not assertive and could easily understand the communication problem. Tom felt sorry for Linda and arranged for another coder. Dr. Baxter, according to Linda, accepted that her deadline would be badly missed but still wanted the work done.

It would have been difficult for Tom to spot the communication problem between Dr. Baxter and Linda by talking to Dr. Baxter alone. The only clue was Dr. Baxter's domineering manner, but that alone wouldn't have much effect without being matched with Linda's submissiveness. The way Tom could have seen it would be to have met with Dr. Baxter and Linda *simultaneously* and carefully watched them interact. When Dr. Baxter said Linda had plenty of time to do the coding, Tom probably could have seen that the expression on Linda's face showed disapproval. Tom could then have asked Linda about her schedule and noticed her tone of hesitancy. Telling Dr. Baxter that it didn't sound like Linda had the time would have either improved their communication or confirmed its hopelessness. At least Tom would have understood the situation better and could have better planned the time and money.

What should you do? The first step is to realize that the problem exists. That is, the person you're talking to may have little or no decision authority and is thus not the real client. The next step is to offer, in your most nonthreatening manner, to tell the messenger that you would be more effective if you could talk directly to any people involved in the study who make decisions involving statistics. Clarify by saying that this includes anyone who has to interpret statistical results. It is vital to offer this without any suggestion of criticism of the client (you won't likely know yet whether you're talking to the client or a messenger) or the messenger. In particular, don't use the word "messenger" to the messenger because of low social status. Use the word "associate" or "colleague." The reason for such delicacy is that the persons you're talking to have absolute power over whether you will be allowed to talk to their superior. Those you're facing must not think you would denigrate them in talking to their boss.

A good share of the time the person you're talking to (who may or may not be the client) is totally undefensive and happy to have you talk to anyone else on the study. If, however, you find that the person you face isn't the decider and you are *not* granted permission to talk to the decider, it's appropriate for you to smell trouble. It may be small or big trouble.

There is more than one reason for the client blocking your access to the decider. For example, take the case of the client who threatened to sue me if I contacted the decider. I knew and respected the decider in that case and think the messenger was a crook who was pulling a fast one on the decider. This is one reason that is infuriating. Another reason for blocking your access to the decider is that the decider thinks the messenger is statistically competent and the messenger isn't confessing that he or she is getting help. This is also upsetting to most statisticians, but it doesn't anger me as much as does the case of the crooked client. (See Chapter 8.)

A third reason for no access to deciders is that they don't realize they have to decide anything and don't want to waste time. You can sometimes overcome this difficulty by telling the messenger that you can make some of the decisions for the decider but are at a loss with others, such as choosing a practical minimum alternative hypothesis or the appropriate power of a test. If deciders hear (from the messenger) that their input is vital and are guaranteed that their time meeting with you won't be wasted, they may well come. If they still won't come, you may have to deal with your own anger at the implication that the decider's time is more valuable than yours or your disrespect for his or her lack of conscientiousness.

If the decider won't meet with you, there are problems. You may not forgive the decider for refusing to meet with you. If you are in a position of power, and angry, you could abort the project in any number of vengeful ways, some more covert than others. Note how far this is from having your purpose aligned with the client's.

Communicating Through Writing

In case you can't meet and talk with the decider, you have to make do with the messenger. It is more complicated and awkward to communicate with the decider through the messenger, but it can be done, and the skill is worth developing. How you do it depends, as always, on your own natural style. One of the main decisions in communication is what to put in writing. The key to knowing how to communicate through a messenger lies in knowing *why* the messenger system is being used. If a messenger is used only to save the decider's meeting time, neither messenger nor decider is defensive; so there are no attitudinal barriers. The problem is then a simple communications problem, in which case you can use your own preferences as to what to say verbally and what to put in writing. It also depends on how good the messenger is at what he or she is supposed to do: carry messages. A statistical message is often very difficult for a nonstatistician to carry; so verbal messages have to be extremely simple and clear.

Messengers come to me with some extremely broad, diffuse instructions from their bosses. They bring messages

like, "How big an n does one need to be statistically significant?" and seem to expect a crisp answer. That is, they expect to carry back only a number, like 10 or 100. What you
want to give them is a list of questions about desired power,
minimal practical alternatives, and required accuracy. These
are too complicated for a messenger to carry verbally and
have to be done in writing. This is a lot of work, but it can be
done if neither messenger nor decider is defensive. In the
long run, writing the questions down may save much time.

Sometimes the client's boss sees you as a gatekeeper
who is going to straighten out the client and make sure she
stays on the straightest track. You will have problems relating to the client if she thinks you are her gatekeeper and not
on her side. A senior consultant described such a case. Three
months after the consulting project was done, the client's supervisor entered the consultant's office and asked for a critical review of the client's final report. He wanted to know
whether the client had done good work and should be promoted. This consultant, on reflection, refused to take part in
this evaluation process. He said that he refused because of
his desire to stick with his client and be someone the client
could trust. He said that he felt the quality of science that
was done in their organization would suffer if the client
could not count on him to be neutral relative to any further
evaluation of the work. He considered it critical to maintain
his client's trust and thought cooperating with the client's
boss would undermine this trust. Remember that this is a
senior consultant who presumably could politically afford
his moral stand. A junior consultant would likely be in a
dilemma.

Jargon.   If the decider and/or messenger *is* defensive,
there are real problems deeper than communication problems. (A problem is a communication problem if communication solves it; the friction between the U.S. and USSR, for
example, will not be solved by communication. It is not a
communication problem.) The messenger's or decider's defensiveness is likely to make you angry. One way to express
your anger is to insist that clients put every request of you in
writing while you respond to every request in writing. Why

is putting it in writing an expression of anger? Putting it in writing doesn't have to be an expression of anger, but it can be. The way to write with anger is to demand that deciders be *very* specific in their instructions while you respond with overqualified answers. We can always demand that our clients be more specific in their objectives than is humanly possible, and we can overqualify our answers with statements like, "The confidence intervals are strictly valid *only if* the parent distributions are Gaussian. . . ." This overqualification of answer is what makes clients of all kinds frustrated at academic statisticians who consult. Of course, no parent distributions in real life are truly Gaussian; so statisticians who give answers this qualified are never responsible. They have left themselves an exit from any responsibility.

In the frustrating situation in which you must work through a messenger who carries statistical complexities back to the decider, writing is essential. Any skill you have in writing is invaluable here. As we just said, it is easy for a statistician to intimidate a client in writing. It's important to be clear and to avoid using technical jargon. Written communication is very different from verbal communication. The main difference is that written communication is preserved forever. It cannot be retracted. Knowing this, we are more guarded in what we write than in what we say. The good side of writing is that written communication is much more thorough. It can be checked over by the sender and the sender's friends before being sent. It can also be reread many times by the receiver. It can be (and in these days of legalistic terror, it is) stored for posterity by both sender and receiver and hauled out at a later date. Knowing this makes senders careful; whether they communicate or obfuscate depends on their skill and intentions. Unless you are particularly skilled at writing, it's wise to have a friend read it over before you give it to the messenger or send it to the decider. It should be read for clarity, freedom from jargon, and tone (helpful versus hostile).

Tone.   Tone is crucial. The letter or memo in a hostile tone, including the subtle hostility people read into a jargon-packed snow job, can be read and reread by the receiver, who then gets angrier and angrier. The receiver can show this to other clients and your boss as proof that you are not a helpful person.

By *tone* we mean a between-the-lines message. The negative tones of memos from statisticians to clients are of two types. They accuse the client of being either stupid or crooked. It's relatively easy for you to reread your own memos to clients and catch your innuendoes that accuse the client of being *crooked*, but it's hard for you to catch the insinuation that the client is careless or a fuzzy thinker. As a matter of fact, that is the main gripe that statisticians have about their clients. Statisticians are frustrated at clients because clients bring messy data and loosely formulated questions. This frustration tempts young statisticians to scold their clients by the subtle, well-intentioned technique of pushing them to be more clearheaded than they can possibly be. This bothers clients because they are vulnerable to the implied criticism. Clients wish they could be more clearheaded, and feel embarrassed that they aren't. They may be embarrassed by having to ask for a consultant's help because it means they have to admit ignorance. They may thus be especially vulnerable to a put-down of their thinking ability in a memo from a consultant they have already refused to meet.

The first line of defense against sending a letter that has a hostile tone or is intimidating with jargon is to examine your own feelings thoroughly. If you are feeling frustrated or hostile toward the client, there's a good chance your memo will show it. If you're feeling negative when you write it, put it aside for a day and read it carefully before you send it. If in doubt, have a friend check it. Why the extra care about tone?

We're dealing with the situation in which you are talking to a messenger who has refused to let you talk to the decider or says the decider won't talk directly. This in itself indicates something is wrong in the relationship, but you can't tell for sure what it is or how bad it is. It's the tip of an iceberg of unknown size. With this warning signal, it's politically wise to be very careful about the *tone* in your writing.

The saving of a client's ego is crucial. Clients are vulnerable to our criticism of their thinking ability and lack of conscientiousness in formulating their questions. We are correspondingly frustrated at messy problems and want to insist clients be as clear as possible. The danger of turning off clients is greatest when you correspond with unseen clients, and you can't read their facial expression as they read your written message.

ALLOCATING RESPONSIBILITIES

Getting it straight as to who is going to do what and when to have it done is natural for statisticians. With our tidy minds, we love good plans, delineation of duties, and mental organization of all kinds. We not only like it; we tend to be good at it. Most of us are better at it than most of our clients. Still, it is a part of consultation that is too often badly done, for reasons all the way from neglecting to do it at all to trying to do it so thoroughly and precisely it creates an overly legalistic atmosphere.

Seldom does a client have the tasks of statistical service categorized and bring them up in orderly fashion for discussion with a statistician. An experienced client may have been through the statistical mill often enough, with bad experiences resulting from miscommunicated responsibilities, to insist on clarity from the start. But such clients are not the rule. You should think about the list of statistical duties and have a plan for allocating them.

It's somewhat arbitrary as to what to call "statistical." The different authors of statistical consulting articles have different opinions about what the statistician should take on and what the client should do. There are very different situations presented to statisticians, particularly as to whether the question is one of design or analysis. (It's very common for a statistician talking to a client who wants an analysis done to start telling the client that the design was wrong. In other words, the client's question is an analysis question but the statistician can't resist giving a design answer. "You should've used a matched pair design, not a randomized design!")

Although there is wide client-to-client variation in what

is to be done, it is important to construct a list of duties, with timetables for completion, and talk it over with the client early in the negotiations. We highly recommend that the beginning consultant, eager to establish a satisfied, satisfying clientele, be responsible for arranging for coding, keypunching, data file construction, and programming. The key question is *how* to negotiate with the client.

Formal Contracts

There is a continuum of formality in talking about the statistical tasks with clients. Deming (1965) wrote one of the most thoroughly thought-out recommendations regarding negotiations with a private client. He presents in detail his view of what a professional statistician is and what responsibilities the statistician has in a consultation. My first reaction to his article was, "I could never say those things to my clients; they are too abrupt." The paper is a long and detailed consideration of many aspects of professional practice. I do not agree with all his recommendations. However, Deming is a very successful statistical consultant and uses his published ideas in his practice. They apparently work for him, and those that you and your client are comfortable with can work for you. The Deming form of agreement demands great clarity in the client-consultant relationship. It is in the form of a contract that both client and consultant sign. It is clearly appropriate to use the formal contract if you are an outside consultant in order to be legalistic and formal in dealing with a large company used to living in the world of labor disputes and competitors' lawsuits. Such companies are suspicious of any consultant who doesn't deal with others in a very businesslike and legalistic manner, covering all bases and contingencies. They may consider other methods of dealing naive and indicative of general incompetence.

However, the very formal and legalistic method appropriate for the experienced, tough client such as a large corporation can disturb other clients. To illustrate, notice the new rules for guaranteeing bill payment for hospitals. Have you tried to enter a hospital, feeling sick and worried, only to be told you must fill out a financial statement before you can be admitted? Many people have. We have. It doesn't fit the image you want to have of hospitals, namely, that they are warm and friendly and much more concerned about your health and comfort than with profits. Their checking your bank balance before they check your health fans your fears that doctors are really greedy entrepreneurs who don't care whether you live or die as long as you pay them.

There is a similar feeling in clients who are statistically vulnerable and hoping desperately to find a statistician who wants to help more than to worry about being cheated by the client. With these clients, there is a very delicate balance between being reassuringly clear and conveying defensiveness. They want you to hear their troubles thoroughly before you get picky about what you will and won't do for them. As a matter of fact, most clients are happiest if you never get picky at all, but just handle it.

Not being up front and direct with clients makes most statisticians uncomfortable. Clarity and specificity are in statisticians' blood, and they want to make every problem a well-defined problem and every client goal clear and crisp. We, too, are in favor of being clear and crisp, but we emphasize the importance of being able to handle it in a gentle manner. Remember that the greatest turnoff for clients is intimidation; so with already intimidated clients, it is especially important for you to *appear* relaxed and friendly in negotiating responsibilities. This is necessary to minimize their fears that you're going to abandon them by dumping problems they can't handle in their lap.

I recently learned a method of negotiating fees that I think would be tolerable to even the most intimidated client. In essence, a lawyer whose counsel I sought told me clearly and without apology her fee structure and policy of having clients put $1,000 in escrow for her. She allowed me ample time to ask questions about the escrow arrangement, and I felt very comfortable with it. ·

Typical Problems

We appreciate that there are problems that really are the client's to solve but for which he or she is unprepared.

For example, in design problems, we always run into the sample size question. Clients expect us to come up with a number that is the official sample size, approved by the ASA for all studies. They think they're asking an easy question, "How big does my n have to be so that the data will be statistically significant?" They aren't prepared for us to turn around and ask them to make some hard decisions. If confidence interval estimation is the technique, then you or the client has to decide on the desired width. You ask most clients how much accuracy they want, and they'll ask you in return how much accuracy they're *supposed* to want. You and the client can go back and forth on this for awhile, and some clients will never understand it. This illustrates the typical duty-allocation difficulties. It is wise not to decide what you will or will not handle until you find out what the client *can* do, let alone wants to do. An infuriating aspect of some clients is that they act as though they feel *above* having to participate in statistical decisions, although such is often a defensive cover for their inability. It is frustrating to find yourself making decisions that the client is supposed to make but can't.

Many times I've given up on getting clients to say what accuracy they need. I feel inadequate to make the decision, but the client is just paralyzed with indecision; so I do it and hope for the best.

In addition to recommending that you don't go into a consultation with a list of things you rigidly refuse to do, we recommend you don't have a rigid order in which you cover your agenda. It gives you a friendlier image to take them in the client's order. Those that don't come up in conversation you can pick up more formally a little later.

We illustrate this by analogy in the style of taking a medical history. A doctor can take your medical history in the classical way by asking you to sit down and relate your aches, pains, and dizziness and then marching you through the whole checklist of childhood diseases. This is appropriate when you are feeling fine and are simply having a physical exam. But if you're away from home in your motel room and start feeling chest pain and left arm numbness for the first time in your life, you want to be seen immediately by an expert and you particularly want assurance you'll be taken care of. You don't want first to methodically and tediously go through a medical history.

The more emotional the state of the helpee, the less able he or she is to be patient with the helper's agenda. Helpers (doctor or statistician) see the relationship as one of work. They want to do the task well, with minimum effort and maximum satisfaction. After helping a few clients, they start to see a pattern and develop their own interview method. When clients are in an emotional state, however, they can't listen to you until they are reassured that you have heard them, in spirit and in letter. If you can be patient enough to listen to your clients' agendas first and skilled enough to convince them you have not only heard their concerns but accept their validity, you will then maximize clients' ability to listen to you. They will keep repeating their message until *they* think, not *you* think, you have heard it. If they think you haven't heard it, they'll keep worrying about how to get it across to you. They'll do this until they think you have heard it and *accept* it. If clients are polite, they'll be silent while you talk but wait for your pauses so they can give you their message again. Only when they think you've got it can they start to relax and listen to you. Of course, you may be in the same state as your client, pressing to make your points and not wanting to listen to them. The difference is that clients are the helpees (guests) and you are the helper (host), and they are supposedly in a more emotional state than you are and more in need of care. (This is not necessarily true, of course. We'll discuss complications of consultant emotion in Chapter 9.)

There is a subtle but vital point to be made here. Listening to clients' concerns (for example, some critic thinks the client has too much missing data) and accepting that they have those concerns does *not* mean you have to take the client's side. You may agree with your client's critic. But it is ineffective to start arguing with clients before *they* think you have heard them.

The point is that if your client's state is at all emotional, do not force a rigid interviewing agenda on him. You may start it, but watch his face and listen to him carefully. If his face contorts and he starts to interrupt, it's better to drop the rigid format and let him talk. You can pull him away from statistical irrelevancies, like too much scientific detail, before you've got the logic airtight, but keep listening for main themes. Is he afraid you're not going to help him? Is he worried there's not enough time or money? Is he embarrassed because he's made a mistake? Is he angry at someone who's hassling him? Such powerful themes can dominate his mind and cloud his thinking and ability to listen to you. It will pay you in the long run to hear him out.

If you encounter clients like these, your first job is to create an environment they perceive as safe and nonthreatening. Having equal chairs and a comfortable, noncluttered space within which to work is useful. Be sensitive to the home court advantage you have established when you meet in your office. Respect the clients' need for a certain amount of space. Do not sit too close. Respect the fact that other individuals may not be able to sit as close to you as comfortably as you can sit close to them. Hold your telephone calls and visitors so that you can focus your attention on the client. Clients feel unimportant if you are repeatedly interrupted by phone calls and visitors. If you think your client is uneasy, it is useful to ask, "What would be helpful for us to do now?"

POLITICS

It's frustrating enough for a statistician to try to make the world a better place by advancing scientific knowledge without all the interferences of human nature. It's one thing to have to deal with your clients and your emotions, but another to face the fact that your clients' success or failure hinges on whether they and their work are in or out of political favor. This may be the applied statistician's most difficult adjustment. You can do an excellent job for a client you respect personally and professionally, only to find that "somebody up there" is against it. You can find that you and your client's report got either buried or misinterpreted and is doomed to company bad-mouthing. On the other hand, there are clients who are terribly fuzzy thinkers, poor planners, and data interpreters of questionable ethics but who lead a charmed political life.

Doing Favored Research

Sometimes clients have connections with somebody in power, but more often the client's area of research is in favor. This can be extreme. I've had clients who seem totally confused about what they're trying to do. All they know is that they're working on a hot topic and collecting all the data on it they can think of. They don't know what they're going to do with it other than "have it analyzed," like policemen have the crime lab "go over the (scene of the crime) room." Such clients often can't tell one statistician from another, other than which ones are friendly and which ones aren't.

All statisticians who keep their eyes and ears open sooner or later run into clients who are very good scientists but who fight losing political battles and clients who are bad scientists but politically blessed. Some of the former are good researchers who try to take on the establishment. For example, my clients who try to do research that questions current medical practice have a terrible time getting permission for clinical studies. The old treatment is so established that no one wants to risk enlisting study subjects for the new treatment. I also have had clients who aren't even interested in research but are assigned to it because the vast amounts of money thrown around created a hyperactive research atmosphere. For example, when former President Nixon declared war on cancer, money was given indiscriminately to good and bad researchers alike who promised to study anything even remotely related to cancer. In such a situation, a statistician can get in on the ground floor by developing a reputation for being "helpful" in a money-rich area and by becoming known to powerful people. This can happen without the statistician having to do anything mathematically profound.

A good example of this happened recently. A young statistician, Don, has a reputation for being a good explainer of statistical phenomena to even unscientific vice presidents in his company. One day he got a call from the vice president of personnel. Don met with her from 5 to 8 P.M., missing dinner, with the VP talking in circles. Don couldn't see a point to the meeting. He remained patient, however, partly because of the VP's power in the company but also because she was a nice person who seemed to want to be sincere and get to some point, if only she knew how. Then, a little after 7:30, Don saw what it was. The VP was trying to solve a linear equation in one unknown. She was dying of embarrassment at her mathematical ineptitude, but had to have help and had been keeping an eye out for someone who would help her without putting her down. She'd decided to ask Don, not directly, but hoping that Don would discover it without the VP having to directly admit her ignorance.

Don handled it perfectly, from psychological and political points of view. He saw what was happening and did his best not to show anger, disappointment, or even surprise. He also did not attempt to teach the VP how to solve such equations in general. Don just solved the equation the VP had and explained the solution in a simple, clear, nonpatronizing manner.

The VP was ecstatic; she told Don he was a genius. She sent a memo to the other VPs of the company, with a copy to Don's boss, saying that Don is an exceptionally good man who is not only a brilliant statistician but really cares about the company and has a bright future as a rapidly promotable executive. She further noted that it is very uncommon to find a statistician who really wants to be helpful, rather than just be picky and critical.

Don's boss promptly called him into his office and asked how on earth Don had developed this key connection. Don says that since the incident his boss is treating him with a suspicious respect for having the high connection. The VP has been absolutely chummy ever since, wanting to talk on and on with Don at the social level.

Look at how much happened from Don having a reputation as a clear, nonpatronizing explainer. He used a combination of tact and political savvy to develop a major company contact. What do you think about the story? It has several aspects. Do you judge Don's behavior to be sleazy and ambitious in the bad sense of the word? He had several options, including calling for remedial math courses for all vice presidents. Can you think of another strategy Don should have used that would better advance the statistics unit in the company? Note that Don focused on getting the job done and using whatever worked. He wisely avoided worrying about who should know what.

Choosing Your Position

Maybe you chose statistics partly because you wanted to get away from people problems in general and political problems in particular. You *can* get away from them in a sense by ignoring them and being generally angry at them. Anger at political problems is most statisticians' response. Statisticians, as a group, see themselves as highly moral-scientific, appointed as the guardians of the scientific method. One of my key statistical mentors told me, totally seriously, that my secondary vocational role is to do statistics, but my primary role is to "resist horseshit."

What stand should you take? Well, your moral-ethical position is pretty well fixed by now; so you're unlikely to have much choice about how you *feel* about politics. You may have some control about what you *do* about political problems, however. As you notice the full spectrum of clients, with some good scientists out of political favor and some bad scientists in political favor, you realize you have choices as to how you allocate your time. As you get full of clients and short of time, you can justify, within wide limits, spending much more time on some clients than on others. If you intensely dislike working with one type, you can give them very little time. But there is a high political risk in being rude to the politically in-favor client. The clearest case occurs when your client is one of your bosses.

My boss's boss is my client. He and my boss negotiate annually and decide on my salary. He also has authority over how big our own biometry department should be. When he is a client, he pays money into our statistics unit. He doesn't always come to me only for statistical advice. He often just wants me to arrange to have something for his administrative unit computerized. He's not cheap, but he wants it error-free and done on short notice. I arrange it for him, often cashing in my chips with other people to meet the short deadlines. He's not a scientist; it's sheer power. I justify my obedience to him on the grounds that our statistics unit (1) needs to survive to be effective, and (2) needs his blessing for our survival. He is extremely pragmatic, and his way of judging whether we are helpful is whether we are helpful to him.

There are much subtler political situations than a nonstatistician higher-up being your client. As a matter of fact, it takes a while on any job, even if you work hard at it, to learn the political network. It's hard to know how a nonstatistician boss of your unit is evaluating it, but chances are it's done in a way statisticians don't like. He or she is probably not finding out who the best scientists are and asking them what they think of the statistics unit. The person is probably a politician and is probably asking people of political power in the company what they think of the statistics unit over which he or she presides. Statistics units are threatening to some people in a company.

This hints at the bind you are in when new clients arrive and you don't know their political connections. Be particularly careful if they see themselves as big shots and seem to you to be bad scientists. The situation is at high risk for you to get angry on both counts (big shot and bad scientist) and use one of the statistician's techniques for "getting" clients. There's a fair chance that if you treat them badly, you will never hear about it directly, but your statistics unit will suffer.

There is a key distinction to make between the politically wise policy of being socially hospitable to all clients until you are sure it is safe to do otherwise and doing whatever clients want you to *technically*. Social hospitality and ethical sellout are *not* the same thing. The mistake is to start arguing with clients about what they want, telling them they don't have the right goal or aren't asking the right questions. There's plenty of time for that later. Take the time to *listen* to their requests and let them know, by repeating them back to the client, that you have heard them and understand them. Only then is it time to say with which of those you can comply and add your own suggestions.

SUMMARY

• Invite your client to discuss time and money allocations *early* in your negotiations. Bring these matters up in your first meeting.

• Keep your client informed as to accumulating costs and unforeseen delays. Submit bills or cross-charges at least monthly.

• Keep on top of the schedules of all the auxiliary services (such as programming) that you use. You are responsible for time and money management of services you delegate.

• The person you're talking to may be the client's messenger and not the client. If so, communicating with the client may be much more difficult. Try to meet at least once with the real client. If you can't, put more information in writing.

• Give every client who seeks your advice at least either a hearing or a referral. Don't keep a potential client waiting for weeks without listening to what his or her situation is.

• Using techniques new to you makes time and money planning more difficult. If you want to use them, explain your desires to the client and obtain his or her consent.

• In allocating responsibilities with your clients, deciding who is going to do what, try to be clear without being overly "legalistic." Don't insist that your clients be very organized if they're not the organized type. Make sure someone on the project is organized.

• Be ready for the impact of company politics on your clients' projects. Your clients' political favor or disfavor often has little to do with the quality of their research. Keep your ear to the ground.

CHAPTER 8

Difficult Clients

At this stage of your life, you have done some categorizing of people into types and know that you prefer certain ones over others. You may have honed this to the degree that you can spot them with little effort and avoid the ones who drive you crazy. You may refuse to categorize people because of racist or sexist implications, but everyone has a hard time *feeling* the same way toward each type of person. For example, it is difficult to take everyone at face value (regardless of race, sex, language, dress, and aggressiveness) and yet not resent bigots.

Hyams (1971) categorized clients. A psychiatrist, he gave reasons for their behaviors and some clues as to which ones are unchangeable. He entitled one "the long-distance runner," a name he gave to the client consumed with personal ambition but having little ability or integrity for careful scientific work. This type of person, according to Hyams, is very insecure because of a deprived childhood and strives desperately for every superficial symbol of success. Assuming Hyams's explanation is correct (we have no reason to doubt it), such clients cannot be shamed by a statistical consultant into becoming more conscientious about the quality of their work as long as they think it makes a good impression on the public. They may just want to be seen by non-researchers as a researcher. They may or may not know the difference between good and bad research; so the reason for their settling for bad research could be lack of conscientiousness or simply ignorance. If they know good from bad, you cannot get them to discuss the details of their work. That is too embarrassing to them.

BAD SCIENTISTS

Bad scientists drive statisticians crazy, and they exist in quantity. As a matter of fact, we seem to have at least one of this type on our active lists at any one time. We've gotten pretty hardened about forming realistic expectations for them and how much energy to put into their projects.

Political Considerations

Working with bad researchers, whether their ineptitude is due to indifference or ignorance, is politically dangerous. Some other people know they're bad researchers, so there's danger of your reputation being tarnished by the association. Because of this, the conservative statistician who can avoid working with these clients will try to do so. These clients are inclined, if they think it will help them, to say loudly that you are their statistician to connote that you (like statisticians are reputed to do) are "keeping them honest." To avoid having your reputation tainted, you need to have an already established reputation of integrity and then hope people will not assume you are selling out to a charlatan.

This raises the issue of whether you can be a good statistician with a client who is a bad scientist. Many statisticians in secure jobs simply shun bad scientists as clients. We think, however, that you can be a good statistician regardless of how bad a scientist your client is and that the problem of taking on a bad scientist is a political, not an ethical, problem. The ethical defense of taking on a bad scientist (we're not talking here about a deliberately crooked client) is the same as the defense of a physician taking on a negligent patient. Consider the patient who is obese, has high cholesterol, smokes two packs of cigarettes a day, and never exercises. He refuses to change any of his health habits and keeps gaining weight. His physician is Dr. Jones. Is Dr. Jones a bad doctor? It depends on what you expect of Dr. Jones. The patient has a shortened life expectancy because of his health habits. If he has to have heart surgery, the surgeon's job is made more difficult by the patient's body fat, and the anesthesiologist's job is complicated by the patient's smoking two packs a day.

You might think that the least Dr. Jones can do is to frighten the patient into better health habits. Health educators might recommend against a scare strategy, however, arguing that increasing his health fears would increase his anxiety level and cause him to use *more* tobacco and food. (There is a parallel in a statistician scolding a bad scientist client who, instead of becoming a better scientist, avoids statisticians or withholds information from them that would provoke further scoldings.) All the patient's uncooperative, self-destructive attitude will allow is that Dr. Jones get some periodic health measurements and bail him out of this or that medical emergency. Dr. Jones can rant and rave to himself and to other doctors about the patient's lack of cooperation and probable early death. Does this lack of influence on the patient make Dr. Jones a bad doctor? No. Dr. Jones's refusing to be this patient's physician won't make the patient better. Similarly, your refusing to be the statistician for bad scientists will not make them into good scientists. Your refusal will also not make them quit doing science. Their options are to do science with or without the help of a statistician. Your job (remember that circumstances have given you this client) is to form realistic expectations for this client and act accordingly.

Realistic Expectations

There is an art to forming realistic expectations for the client who is a bad scientist. Many such clients are not all that bright, and it's a waste of your time and energy to try to explain anything but a simple graph to them. (Even the bright client can often understand surprisingly little statistical reasoning.) With such clients, don't torture yourself about their limitations and what you can do for them.

One of my clients stands out when I think of the bad scientist client who means well. He has a large data set that he keeps massaging in trying to carry out his regulatory job. The quality of the data is not good because institutions he's trying to regulate fudge their input into the data set to avoid being caught and thus regulated. He could disregard the data and just regulate by the seat of his pants, but he sincerely believes in the scientific method, including computers and staisticians. I've been working with him for years. Every time he hears about a new statistical technique, he insists his data be subjected to it. He always asks me what I think of it. I usually say I don't think it would be appropriate, or more appropriate than the technique I keep trying to talk him into. He insists on it being done; so I arrange to get it done for him. After it's done, he comes in demanding to know why it gives a different answer than the last technique he tried. I try to explain why, but fail. A month later, he comes back with another hot idea for analysis. He's even come full circle and wants techniques used he already used before. He has high ego strength, and I've told him he's wasting his (the government's) money with all the analyses when he hasn't got some basic definitions straight. He has a thick skin; so I tell him what I think, but I no longer get worked up with frustration over his refusal to take my original recommendation. I think he's better off than being without a statistician, at least to keep him from overinterpreting some of the wild answers he gets from the more irrelevant analyses.

DOMINEERING CLIENTS

Another kind of client that is hard for statisticians to handle is the domineering client. We're not considering here the double problem of clients consumed with their own sense of self-importance who are *also* bad scientists. The client type we're talking about is a good scientist but has conspicuous ego needs that can cause a statistician to think more about revenge than assistance.

I vividly recall my first client of this type. A young research physician burst into my office. I was alone at the time and she acted as though whatever I was doing was not as important as what she was about to instruct me to do. She was a messenger for her boss, Dr. T, a physician of world renown whose name I had frequently heard. The messenger wanted me to do an analysis that I thought was inappropriate. I refused to do it without explaining my reservations to Dr. T. She then left, promising to relay the message. About fifteen minutes later, I saw Dr. T stride vigorously past my office door with the messenger hot on his heels, headed straight for the office of my boss, Al. Dr. T entered Al's office in a manner that said Al should drop whatever he was doing and listen to Dr. T's complaints about me. Al asked me to join them. Dr. T reminded Al that he and Al never had any trouble working together; so why not just bypass me and get it done right, like Dr. T wanted it in the first place? Dr. T told Al that Al had used that analysis on similar data before. Al was in a bind, partly because of Dr. T's political power. Al was sensitive to political problems, but he wanted to defend me. To complicate it further, Al and I had some honest difference of opinions on how Dr. T's data should be analyzed. Al was a more experienced statistician than I, but he tolerated our difference pretty well. He tried his best to smooth it over, hoping to placate both Dr. T and me.

I don't think Dr. T heard anything Al said. As soon as he said his piece to Al, he took the first opportunity to storm out of Al's office, data in hand and the young physician-messenger trailing close behind. Neither Al nor I ever heard from Dr. T professionally again, though I saw him in the halls for the next ten years. He never again acknowledged my presence.

What had happened? I started to get some gossip on Dr. T. Everyone confirmed that he was an outstanding researcher in his specialty and deserved his international reputation. They also agreed that he has no sense of humor about anything and takes both himself and his work absolutely seriously. At every opportunity, he reminds people of his contributions to knowledge. My informants also told me whenever he and his wife appear socially in public, she always addresses him by *title*, not his first name, even when talking directly to him. We speculated how she addressed him privately.

What I had done to Dr. T psychologically is what psychiatrists call narcissistic insult. A person of my low level not only refusing to carry out his order but arguing with the wisdom of his order hit him right in his self-concept. His authority was questioned by an inferior and he couldn't take it.

Avoiding Power Struggles

This kind of client is very difficult for most statisticians. They are very good scientists, but the statistician has to deal with their ego problems. Many statisticians can't take it and, if given the choice, tell such clients off. It's tempting with these clients to do a slow burn and take them on in a power struggle, giving them trouble at every opportunity. Statisticians have many tricks for putting clients down, ranging from chipping away with suggestions that the client is a careless planner or a sloppy thinker all the way to taking excessive time to do the analysis and overqualifying the report.

We recommend against getting into a power struggle with the domineering client, at least as a first effort. Our recommendation is to do just the opposite. Domineering clients are very insecure about their status. It is their most sensitive area. They are extremely uncomfortable in any situation in which their status is questioned and can relax and work on other things only when they don't have to keep proving their status. They will keep telling you in as many ways as they can that they have high status and will not concentrate well on other matters until you get the message. We recommend you give them the message that you recognize and accept their high status. If they believe you are impressed, they will function at their maximal intellectual and social capacity.

Carrying this out may tie your stomach in a knot. It could make you dysfunctionally furious. However, it offers the most hope for improving the clients' attitudes and focusing their attention on the task at hand. What about your own attitude? Can you take it?

There are two saving graces to treating domineering clients by giving them the social strokes they want. First, most of the clients who demand recognition of their status *have* high status. Thus, reassuring them that you see they have high status isn't a lie. Second, once you reassure them, they are more willing to accord high status to you because their defensiveness is reduced.

Diagnosis

How do you diagnose the domineering client? Their symptoms can take various forms, depending on their social sophistication. People seldom come in simply one-dimensional types; so indications that they're domineering clients are often confounded with other personality signs. Keep your ears open for their boasting about accomplishments, connections with important people, authority over many people, lots of money at their fingertips, and high value on their personal time. As a treatment plan, respond to whatever they say. For example, if one says, "I used to know Albert Einstein," respond with something like, "Einstein was a genius." You don't have to go overboard and get nauseating with, "Only really important people knew Einstein." If one mentions how much money he or she controls, say "That's good to hear. We can then use the best design without worrying about the budget." If one mentions the importance of his or her time, say, "I'll try to bother you only for key decisions." Your comments should be essentially honest, but be sure to touch on the area of concern. If you watch and listen to them carefully, you should see or hear signs of their relaxing, and then you can settle down to the scientific task at hand.

There is another, more subtle way to diagnose this kind of client. Simply pay attention to how you are feeling socially toward them. If you somehow feel put down, it's time to become more alert to the message they're sending you. It could well be a little body language here or a condescending tone there that's putting you off. Notice whether you're getting distracted and starting to think of ways of putting this client in his place. This method of monitoring your own tension level works in other settings more or less well, depending on your social sensitivity. The insensitive consultant won't notice or get angry at the put-down message of the domineering client; so the *statistician* won't be bothered or distracted. These *clients*, however, won't be able to think or cooperate maximally until the statistician recognizes their high status.

INDECISIVE CLIENTS

I can't recall, even to the nearest fifty, how many times a client has come to see me with a childlike faith that big computers and big statistics can see all and do all with numbers. Such clients' faith is frightening as their unrealistic expectations unfold before your eyes. These clients may be good or bad scientists, but they typically are not great conceptualizers. In pure form, they are sincere and well intentioned. They tend to be naive and presume other people have good motives unless dramatically proved otherwise. They believe in experts in general and well-credentialed statisticians in particular. Now what could be nicer than to have a client who is obedient and reveres your expertise? How nice it is depends on whether you need the client to make a decision.

Making Clients' Decisions

Overly reverent clients think you can receive the data and go off to analyze it without any input from them. They are at a loss, after they have asked you what sample size they ought to have, when you start asking them about the goals for their research and what questions they are trying to answer. We statisticians know that well-formulated questions are difficult to answer. We really can't provide answers for nonquestions, but that is what indecisive clients ask us to do.

Some clients simply bring us data to be "analyzed" with only vague goals, such as to "see if there's anything going on." When pressed to the limit, they will go so far as to say to "try to find if there's any significant correlations" or "compare the new method with the old method." It is frustrating to work with them because of their inability or unwillingness to make the decisions necessary for well-formulated questions. They're like the patient who tells the doctor, "You're the doctor. You tell *me* where it hurts!"

Indecisive clients aren't necessarily bad scientists. They are often extremely conscientious in their research. They are not good with abstract concepts, have never learned even the most basic statistical concepts, or were perhaps burned by too bold decision making. Indecisive clients are that way for one reason or another, but the effects on you are similar: they expect you to make decisions they should be making.

A client came to me after she had collected data on job satisfaction of two occupational groups. She had asked by mail questionnaire each worker in the two groups eighty questions regarding satisfaction and had assigned numbers 1, 2, 3, 4, 5, ranging from strongly disagree to strongly agree, to the answers. She wanted to know if there are any differences between the two groups. I tried to explain that, in the populations of the two groups of workers, there must be *some* differences in job satisfaction on *some* variables. I went on to say that even if we didn't get statistical significance on any of the variables, it still wouldn't mean there are no differences (in population averages). She looked blankly at me. (I decided not to try to explain deeper problems, such as the multiple inferences problem requiring omnibus tests or simultaneous confidence intervals. Even with clients who are good at concepts, I have little success explaining multiple inference problems.)

I then asked if she had an idea of how big a real difference in the *two populations* would be of practical importance. She didn't know what I meant. I said, "For example, if the highly educated workers had a mean satisfaction of 3.4, and the less educated had a mean of 2.9, would that be an important amount, causing someone to take action or even take particular note?" (She wanted to use means even though I encouraged the use of medians.) She then said, "If their satisfaction isn't at least 3.5, there's something wrong." I followed this tangent and asked whether she wanted to compare the two groups or just see if both are satisfied enough. She said, "Yes, but I also want to compare the two groups to see if there are any significant differences." I asked if she meant practical significance or statistical significance. She said she didn't understand. I gave her my usual speech on the distinction. After I stopped, she said nothing. I tried every explanation I know about to separate statistical and actual significance, but nothing worked. She stuck to her guns and each time returned to her original request, "to see if there's anything significant." I gave up trying to explain.

I was faced there with the decision as to whether to do univariate .05 tests on all eighty variables or two-sample multivariate nonparametric tests. The latter would be preferable theoretically, but the client would still want to know which ones of the eighty are significant. No matter what I did, the client wasn't going to understand the multiple inference problems. She wasn't even going to understand the distinction between practical and statistical significance. All she knew is that there are people called statisticians who analyze numbers, and they're people worth going to when you've got numbers you don't understand. She had faith and she wanted help.

Client Dependency

Indecisive clients could also be called dependent clients. Some statisticians can't stand this type. The clients seem inadequate. It's tempting to tell them they *can't be* clients because they haven't defined the problem. In fact, it seems like they don't even understand what they're doing or why they're doing it. This can have several negative effects on the statistician.

Statisticians like clarity and specificity. They dislike chaos and like to create order. They see science as the noble pursuit of trying to learn the pattern of the universe and admire scientists. They are frustrated by people who impede science or are confused or indecisive. Thus, the indecisive client may not have the statistician's respect. Clients can perceive this disrespect and consequently lack the willingness to cooperate. The statistician is also likely to be afraid to make the decisions he or she thinks are the client's responsibility.

Sample Size Dilemma. This fear of making the wrong decision is heavy for the statistician, who is psychologically compelled to be precise and correct. It's hard enough trying to be statistically correct without being responsible for making decisions the client is supposed to make. It occurs very often in the sample size question. Clients want to know what sample size they should have without even describing the study. When you probe for what are meaningful alternatives, what power is desired (for tests), what are the relative costs of the two types of errors (for tests), what accuracy is needed (for estimates), indecisive clients are of little help. Your options are limited. How can *you* decide?

The sample size question for the indecisive client is tough, but there is help available from the real world. There is a practical upper bound and a practical lower bound. The upper bound is determined by the resources available. The sample size costs something, and the bigger the n, the bigger the cost. The cost as a strictly increasing function of sample size has many components, including data storage and analysis, although the main costs are usually in data collection.

Upper Bound.   Ask the client what is the biggest n she could possibly do. She probably won't hesitate to give you a number. This works for me; it is surprising how boldly and decisively even the indecisive client gives it.

Lower Bound.   Establishing the practical lower bound is more difficult. The practical lower bound is the number the client's audience says is the lower bound. That audience may be a supervisor or a community of scientists or a journal. It is some person or group of people who won't believe the results if the sample size is below what they think it ought to be. That belief isn't well founded or rational. It's simply the belief of a person who has the power to impose it. I remember when I first saw it.

A superbly credentialed client came to see me. He had two doctoral degrees and was known widely for his exacting scientific standards. To get an observation, he had to treat a rat and then have a laboratory technician kill it. His lab techs respected him but thought he was using too many rats, about a thousand per experiment. He did two-way factorial experiments with several treatments per factor and gave me the data from the most recent experiment. I calculated good estimates of variances and treatment effects and thus was able to do some power calculations. In the previous experiment, he had used ten rats per cell and I was proud to announce that in the next experiment he would have plenty of power if he were to use only three rats per cell. I thought he would be delighted.

He wasn't. He was upset. He told me most emphatically, pounding his fist on my desk, that he would have none of it. He said, in a loud and irritated voice, "Listen! I don't believe in experiments that don't have at least ten observations per cell." I tried to reason with him, but to no avail. Ten, for him, is the unarguable minimum.

I also have a client who believes ten is sufficiently large for everything. She sends messengers to see about this or that statistical point because she delegates many studies. In conversing with them, I find that she is still telling them to run their studies with ten subjects. One messenger told me that he wanted to use twenty subjects, but the boss said that would be a waste of subjects. "If you can't answer the question with ten subjects, it doesn't have a clear answer," she said.

Another client asked me if I thought it would work to evaluate a screening program for a rare disease if he did the evaluation using two thousand subjects. I did some calculations that led me to tell him he would need twenty-five thousand subjects. He said, "Well, alright, I'll do three thousand." He went away and I never heard from him on this point again.

Ask the Clients.   I've found it interesting to poll people about their sample size beliefs. When I get into the sample size question with a research team and want to show them how variable the beliefs are, I ask them to give me a piece of paper with "their number" on it. There are a few statistically sophisticated clients around who know all the factors on which sample size depends and thus know that there isn't "a number," but most will write down their number quickly. Most give very round numbers like ten or one hundred, but some demand thousands. The interesting moral with regard to consultation is that those number beliefs are real and relevant, no matter how irrational their basis.

Many times the sample size problem is solved by the fact that the practical upper and the practical (psychological) lower bound are so close together that it makes little difference whether you choose the upper bound, lower bound, or anything in between.

With the sample size trapped between the practical lower bound and the practical upper bound, you have one remaining question. Is the upper bound too low, so that even doing as big a study as the client can, the power of the test will be too low or the estimates will be too inaccurate? In principle, this is the appropriate question to ask. In practice, brace yourself for the unpleasantness of the answer. Whether the study is worth doing, even with the practical maximum sample size, raises the question of the importance of the client's field and how else he or she could spend the time. In other words, it raises many more tough questions. Anyway, it is usually answered by the fact that somebody *insists* that it be done.

A microbiologist came to see me, as she was told to by her supervisor. She asked me if I thought she was using the correct sample size. In her studies, she used five agar plates. We went through the discussion establishing practical upper and lower bounds. Both bounds were five; she had also been doing five. She showed a little sense of humor about this irony of asking about the number when it was the only number she could do. Her mood seemed good and light; so I told her the only decision left was whether to do it at all. She assured me quickly that her boss insisted. I know her boss and the client knew I knew him well. We both understood. The boss is a bad scientist but insisted on this ritualistic visit.

Sometimes the practical upper limit sample size is too small and the client has the option not to do the study and is open to advice from you. Be careful, though, how you suggest that the study not be done because it cannot be done well enough. Many clients are heavily committed to their work and are very defensive about it.

The sample size problem is just one area, although the most common one, you are likely to run into with this client. The indecisive client is a tough one for many statisticians to handle. However, a fair proportion of clients are clearly indecisive and dependent, and almost all clients need some help on decisions you think they ought to make. If you're going to develop into a general statistical consultant and like it, you need to be able to help clients make decisions. It is frightening to stick your neck out and help, but in many cases either you help clients or they don't get help. In some cases, clients will think you are generally wiser than they and undefensively ask your advice.

Your Reward.   There is a powerful psychosocial reward available to the statistician who can work with an indecisive, dependent client. It is the feeling of being a rescuer. Statisticians aren't generally motivated to be rescuers of helpless, dependent creatures, but some of us find it rewarding. Indecisive clients, if treated well by statisticians, can become dependent on them, praising them highly to others and benefiting them politically. We recommend the budding statistician learn to work with indecisive clients. They are the plurality of difficult clients, but mean well and try hard. Many of them, matched up with a statistician who'll make the extra effort, can do from fair to good science.

CROOKS

Crooks are a special kind of difficult client whose very title is a turnoff. Of course, you are against them and have every intention of turning them over to the authorities, who will then administer justice. This would be very simple if all data crooks had low foreheads and beady, darting eyes. You could spot them right away and never get involved in the criminal world. The problem with crooks is that at first impression they seem like the rest of us. As a result, the statistician is already involved before he or she realizes the client is a crook.

Crimes

Crooks knowingly, blatantly misrepresent the data. They rationalize the crime by saying they "know" how the study should have come out and that including all the data would just confuse the reader.

I recall one client crook vividly. He was in charge of a human services program in which he wholeheartedly believed. Someone was asked to arrange a panel discussion to discuss the merits of the human service. The panel consisted of four service recipients, two of whom testified that the service was vital to them; the other two said they could take it or leave it. Somehow the word got out that a study had been done, and it showed that 50 percent of the people need the service. I told the client, whom I know very well, that he should set the record straight and tell the world that a good needs assessment should be done. He disagreed. He said it's too easy to get bogged down in statistical details. He said there's a great need for the program and more good than harm is being done by the "50 percent result." "Leave well enough alone," he said. I saw in print a year later that the need rate was 80 percent. I did some checking and found the 80 percent was just a misquote of the 50 percent. I called the client and pushed him hard on the point, but he never yielded. He thought I was just hung up.

Most of the time the problem is much more subtle. Unlike aggressive treatment of the passive client (such as a surgeon working on the unconscious, unidentified wino brought into the emergency room after a bad fall), we have to have our clients' cooperation. They control what we see and what we hear of their work. What's to keep them from showing us their best numbers? Nothing, unless you have a written agreement explicitly forbidding it. Honest clients simply may not think to tell us or show us certain data or design decisions. It's up to us to probe. In the case of crooks, our probing will have to be more clever; crooks will withhold the sleazy parts of the study or plans to misrepresent the data.

We have clients that we're not sure should be called crooks. Often they will simply refuse to interpret the data analysis the way we recommend. We frequently caution clients not to get their audience excited when they calculate one hundred correlations and find five of them statistically significant. We tell them that even if there's nothing going on, they should expect five or so spurious statistical significances. We go on to say that the five that are statistically significant this time would not be the five that would be significant the next time. This speech usually wins us blank looks, followed by a statement that they just want to know which variables are significant. We've even begged and pleaded for them not to publish those test results without seriously cautioning the reader, but we're usually ignored. The clients go on to gleefully publish the results, not cautioning readers in the least, but drawing their attention to the exciting new significant correlations.

Is such a client a crook? In some of those cases, we know the clients think we're experts in statistical interpretation. When they don't hide from us what they do with the analysis, even though we make it very clear (we think) that we are absolutely against their doing it, it's hard to say whether they're crooks. One view is simply that they see themselves in open, honest disagreement with us.

There are others, though, who see us as statistical experts but walk out of our offices and do precisely what they had agreed not to. We think of them as crooks, and clearly so. Do we call the cops? Not usually. Spotting crooks is one thing; doing something about them is another.

The crime clients commit is usually one of omission rather than commission. That is, they tell some of the truth, but not all of your truth. For example, you discover that the experimental units were not assigned to the treatments at random. The method was "sort of" random, but you're genuinely worried about biases. You do an analysis, but say that it is valid only to the extent that the selection method is random. In other words, the more random, the more valid. You prep the client as best you can. How can you stop clients from ignoring your qualifying remarks? You can offer to look at their written report and delete it if you catch it, but usually you just can't do anything. It's part of being a statistician. This lack of control over clients, with fears that they will misunderstand or cheat, keeps many statisticians from becoming consultants, and it keeps those who *are* consultants more or less uneasy. Clients *do* misunderstand and some *do* cheat. We can minimize it but we cannot eliminate it. Remember that being too suspecting and legalistic creates a chilly atmosphere that scares off many clients. The art is to be friendly without being weak and selling out, but accepting the fact that you're frequently going to be misunderstood and occasionally taken.

We note that this is yet another argument for simplicity of analysis and design. Simplicity decreases misunderstanding and better nails crooks because it weakens their defense, when caught, that they didn't understand.

Punishment

One reason for the difficulty of doing something about crooked clients is that you don't usually find them out until it's pretty late in the game. Crooks don't tell you they're crooked. You find out later, by a paper they published or a report they wrote, that they broke an agreement with you. Unless you energetically follow up your clients, you are not likely to know what they say or write. There is the additional problem that they quote you as their authority.

Sometimes crooks will blatantly contradict something you thought you had made perfectly clear. They say it absolutely backwards. You then have the goods on them. It's hard to get a criminal convicted, though. Al Capone was one of America's best known mobsters. I recall seeing in a newspaper that his personal take from his rackets of prostitution, dope, gambling, and protection was $2 million per week. And that was when he was only twenty-nine years old. What did they get him on? Tax evasion. The FBI couldn't pin the other crimes on him. The moral here is that the case against the crook has to be very good before you can get a conviction.

Put It in Writing

The problem of dealing with crooks is one of the best arguments for getting everything in writing. This means that you get written statements from clients as to what they want done, and they get a written response from you (you keep copies, of course) about everything. Then, when they do what you specifically told them not to, you at least have it in writing and can show it to the "jury."

Getting everything in writing is a good thing to do when dealing with suspects. As a *general* policy, however, it has some drawbacks. A more or less minor drawback is that it takes time. For you to write it and get through the typing pool may take a couple of days. A couple of days is not usually crucial, but sometimes it is. A virtue is that it makes you clarify your own thoughts as you put them down on paper. The main drawback to demanding everything in writing from the client is that some clients interpret your insistence that they write it down as a very unfriendly gesture. Think how you would feel if you were in pain and frightened, but the doctor insisted you put all your complaints in writing. First of all, it's not easy to do. Just as you and I don't think we should have to be articulate about medicine to be a patient, some of our clients are very afraid of statistics and would much rather talk to a friendly, helpful statistician who will listen and interpret their requests. Many clients are afraid of looking foolish, and pressing them to write is pressing them to be more articulate than they think they can be. Having everything in writing has its good side: clarity. Pressing too hard for it gives a tone of distrust.

PERSONALITY CLASHES

There are problems that occur with clients that are not the fault of the client or the fault of the statistician. There is nothing wrong with either person. There is something wrong with the relationship. We commonly see two very good people who made the mistake of getting married to each other. Some consulting problems are like that.

Do you pay much attention to what makes you like or be comfortable with other people? Are you aware of strong preferences for one type of person over another? Are you aware of the cues you emit, showing people your comfort or discomfort? The dynamics of one-to-one interaction between two people is a vast area of study. We'll go into some of them in Chapter 9. For now we simply touch on high points.

Assertiveness

There are key areas to watch for in personality clashes. A major one is assertiveness. Shy, modest, soft-spoken persons might admire bold, loud-talking, domineering persons, but more often they resent them. Those of the former type will frequently see themselves as sensitive and intelligent and see the latter type as a loud, pushy idiot. Persons of the latter type see themselves as being open and direct and see the apparent lack of self-confidence of the former as a sign of incompetence. After all, to the assertive person, "If you've got it, flaunt it!" Neither of these people is "bad," but the natural resentments of one toward the other detract from the relationship.

There are many statisticians who are shy, reserved intellectuals. I have picked up in conversations their resentment of loud, pushy types. A couple of statisticians I know speak barely above a whisper. On the other hand, I recall one client whom I'm sure I turned off who probably saw me as a garish, show-business type. Lew quit coming to me. He is an incredibly conscientious, dedicated scientist. He is always worried and working hard. He frets about every detail and is constantly anguishing about something that's going wrong or that could go wrong. Lew used to come to me pretty frequently, but the last time, I blew it. As usual, he was torturing himself about whether the *assumptions* of the analysis I had done were correct. I told him that the technique is robust and that I wasn't worried. Then I said we didn't have to do a formal analysis anyway because his results were so dramatic they would be convincing. We could do it with a graphical display of the data.

I thought the graph would solve the dilemma. With sharp, definitive results like Lew's, a graph could do it all. Certainly, no editor would nit-pick over it, and it would get Lew out of his bind about assumptions. I was wrong. It wasn't the editor who objected; it was Lew. "Displays!" he exclaimed with great disgust, *"I can't stand displays!"* I've never seen anyone more turned off. His face was totally pinched. What a bomb. I tried to recover and assure him that it is good statistics when one has sharp results like his. "It is also very honest," I said. This last point helped him some, but he never appeared to recover totally. We couldn't agree on what to do, and Lew never came back. I still see him around, and he recognizes me socially. I imagine he's still active in research, but I suppose he now thinks of me as too "show business" oriented to be in science.

Conscientiousness

It is difficult for two people to work together if they have sharply contrasting attitudes regarding whether to do many things pretty well, depending on how much effort they deserve, or take on few commitments and do them very conscientiously. (The latter view is strongly espoused by statisticians in public writing or speaking.) Because you are a statistician, you can undoubtedly think of many people you couldn't stand to work with simply because they are too sloppy and careless. I'm always nagging (or wanting to nag) my son about picking up his room, or spilling food, or putting the tools away wet. I also want him to keep up with his homework. Naturally, he resents all this and tells me to get off his back. We know each other well, and when circumstance dictates our working together, we brace ourselves. I work hard to not criticize or even frown, and he does his best to not blow his stack and walk off the job, telling me again that I'm impossible to work with.

I do this to some clients, too. One I like to work with, Ray, is a bioengineer. He does great experiments, designed without my (or any statistician's) help. He is very careful, has no missing data, and uses good (for a nonstatistician) designs. I keep offering to help with the next design, and he promises to accept my aid, but he never does. He came up just last week and wanted some quick-and-dirty calculations done. He had another good design, a factorial with replicated measurements I was itching to analyze. His work is so much cleaner than most of the stuff I see. He said, "That might be nice, but I'm just interested in main effects. You make too big a deal out of trivia."

There may also be people in your life who are too fussy for you to enjoy working with. We say "may" because statisticians are already necessarily fussy. I do some target shooting with rifles and enjoy making rifles and ammunition more accurate, but some target shooters drive me nuts. They spend way too much time and money making their equipment work well, when the dominant component of variance is their own physical shakiness. Some of them even seem to understand my statistical argument that they're working on the wrong component of variance, but admit they just love fussing.

I see clients who are too fussy. One, Marie, gets upset over missing data at the rate of one observation in a thousand. I assure her that that low a rate can be handled statistically, but she doesn't believe me. She collects so much data on everything that it's a nightmare to keep it straight. She likes me personally, and I don't think she's seeing another statistician on the side (even my best friends probably wouldn't tell me), but I'm sure she thinks I don't worry enough.

Another client, Bert, left me because I resisted doing all the analyses he wanted. He talked to every professional and amateur statistician he could find and got a wide variety of recommendations as to what to do. Bert asked to do them all. I said I could arrange to have them all done if he wanted to spend the money, but it would take more time and create a dilemma. I could see that there was such a wide spectrum of analyses recommended to him that they would likely yield some different conclusions. I told him he would need to decide which one was "correct," and it would be too tempting to call correct the one that gave the answer he liked best. I went on to say that most of the analyses recommended to him were inappropriate anyway and suggested he narrow the list to the few appropriate ones. He said that it's more conscientious and better science to do them all and see what happens. I referred Bert to another statistician who likes to do many different analyses on the same data.

The question of matching on conscientiousness is an important one. It's a tough area because most adults are well programmed into a particular spot on the conscientiousness scale. A major basis of humor in the show *The Odd Couple* is a clash between a neatnik and a slob. Every audience member clearly identifies with one of the actors more than with the other and can feel deeply for his frustration. What can you do when you and the client are far apart in conscientiousness?

If your client is not conscientious enough for you, you may be inclined to see it as an ethical problem, viewing him or her as a bad scientist. You may think you are wasting your time and talent and fear that the association will taint your reputation. It's a tough situation. Your first step is to push for more thoroughness. If that doesn't succeed, and it usually doesn't, the decision is whether to lower your standards of thoroughness to the client's and do something relevant but quick and dirty.

I have come to do the latter, and put just as much effort into the client as I think he or she can handle—that is, provided there aren't major ethical problems. I rationalize this policy of giving a little help to the rushed, apparently shallow client as follows. I would rather that every scientist who seeks the help of a statistician get *some* help than statisticians save themselves for "good" clients. This is a very subjective value judgment that I defend, but I appreciate that it is wide open to attack. It's quite an art to have a quick-and-dirty consultation and feel good about it. But more often than not, I feel more good than harm was done.

HARRIED CLIENTS

Some clients, especially those in a great rush, tend to skip explaining the problem. Typically, they will start a session with a proposed solution. "I have just one question that I want you to answer for me. Shouldn't I perform ANOVA on this data set?" We support endorsing a client's solution to a problem *if* it is at all appropriate. In fact, we strongly favor encouraging such independence and initiative on the part of the client. However, it is risky to not understand the situation, even though the client wants to talk about solutions immediately. Before you can assess the wisdom of clients' proposals, you must somewhat understand their problem and the goal of their investigation.

One of the common ways this problem presents itself is when a client pokes her head into your office and asks you what you think of her solution. There is a great temptation on all our parts to want to appear quick of wit and swift on our feet. Thus, it is tempting to give a quick answer. We recommend saying something like, "On the surface that sounds plausible, but I don't know enough about what you are trying to do to give you a thoughtful answer. Why don't we set up an appointment to explore that?" This often is not what the client is looking for, but your alternative is to make a wild guess as to the appropriateness of the client's solution.

There *are* clients who refuse your offer because (1) they are too rushed or (2) they don't want you to know more about their work. Some clients ask you to approve an action of theirs while avoiding letting you know anything about the goals of their investigation or the situation in which they are operating. You cannot force clients to share information about their situation or goals with you. A response of friendly confrontation may be necessary in which you kindly but firmly state that it is impossible for you to answer the client's question effectively without additional information regarding the situation in which the question arises and the overall goals of the research program. You can explain that to answer the question without this information would make your answer shallow and possibly flatly wrong. Promise confidentiality. Secretive clients will often cooperate if they see that the information is essential for you to be help-ful.

POTENTIALLY CONFOUNDING CHARACTERISTICS

Age

The relative ages of the consultant and client affect the success of the consulting session. Age partly defines status. If you are a young statistical consultant, some of your clients will be as old as your parents or even grandparents. This age gap can pose attitudinal difficulties. It may be awkward for you to criticize even implicitly the thinking of a person who is as old as your father and perhaps reminds you of him in some ways. Dealing with older clients can be difficult if you have trouble with authority figures. Some consultants defer to authority figures; others rebel against them. Rebellion may cause the older person to perceive you as having a chip on your shoulder and avoid additional consulting sessions with you.

I tend to defer to authority figures, but the rebel in me gets angry at this deference. I am upset by this but continue to make progress on the problem by dealing with it on a con-scious level. Sensitivity to age and sex can manifest itself in a variety of ways. To illustrate, one quarter I decided to start my class by shaking hands with everyone and introducing myself as they came into the room. I insisted upon learning the names of and shaking hands with every male who en-tered the classroom and all the females who were younger than I. However, there were three females who were about ten to fifteen years older than I in the class, and for one rea-son or another, I managed to not shake their hands, despite my decision to shake everyone's hand. This indicates my def-erence or fear of these individuals and leads me to realize that if I encountered an older woman as a client, I might avoid her in some important way.

Sex

I experience discomfort with certain male clients. If the client is about my own age, extroverted, competitive, athletic looking, and a competent statistical methodologist in his own field, I have noticed that I have a tendency to be critical and evaluative of his work. My behavior was worse when I was unaware of it and didn't understand the competitiveness such an individual triggers in me. Now that I know what's happening, I can better control my own negative behavior.

Race

Sometimes the difference in the races of the consultant and client poses a problem. I continue to have traces of "white man's guilt," which I notice affects me occasionally with black clients. It manifests itself as my unwillingness to terminate a session with a black client before I feel that I have given him or her enough statistical reward for coming to see me.

Nationality

Another factor that can affect the consulting session is the nationalities of the consultant and client. Some difficulties can occur if the two are from different countries. These difficulties arise more often as more scientists from outside the United States enter this country's scientific job market. If you are dealing with clients from other countries, think about your stereotypes and theirs. Often, your definitions of polite behavior differ. Make *sure* that the verbal messages that are exchanged are understood. If in doubt, put them in writing. We recommend that you frequently repeat tactfully what clients have said and that you ask them to repeat one of your suggestions. It is not effective to ask the clients if they have understood your suggestions. Clients from "polite" cultures always say yes no matter what. It is necessary to get a playback from them. If their English is not fluent and they speak rapidly, ask them to speak slowly. This is awkward, but better than risking misunderstanding what clients have said.

SUMMARY

• You can be a good statistician even with a bad client. The secret is to have realistic expectations for the relationship.

• Different types of clients need different kinds of handling.

• Be aware of the types of people you dislike and how you behave with them, and work on developing a constructive style of interaction.

• Don't expect clients to change much, even when they see how you would like them to behave. Take them as they are.

CHAPTER 9

Dataside Manner

Certainly you've heard of bedside manner. It is what physicians do with reassuring warmth to soothe patients. The image is that the patient is in pain and frightened, lying in bed. He thinks of his physician as medically competent as well as caring. He hangs on every word the physician utters and watches her like a hawk to see if she is worried. The patient scrutinizes not only the physician's words and their literal meaning, but every wrinkle around her eyes, the arch of her back, and her tone of voice. The patient is desperately trying to hear good news from the physician and dreading bad news.

The patient's antennae are finely tuned to the physician, straining to hear the prognosis. What he hears will affect not only his morale, but his ability to listen to the physician's prognosis. For example, if the patient is worried that he has cancer, hearing from the physician that he has cancer will likely overwhelm him emotionally so that he can't hear what *else* she says. If the physician says that the cancer is extremely mild and that the patient has many good years of life remaining, the emotional patient will filter the news, hearing only that he is going to die a horrible death soon or blocking out the bad news and hearing only the phrase "many good years of life." Even in much milder issues between physicians and patients, emotions diminish ability to think clearly.

The physician who is good at reassuring patients is said to have a good bedside manner. We want our physicians to have the ability to reassure us when it is appropriate. We may even want them to to be reassuring when there isn't much cause for reassurance, realizing that in a medical crisis we may do better by not knowing the whole truth.

THE EFFECT OF EMOTIONS

Statisticians can see through a syrupy reassurance very quickly and are leery of con artists. The phrase "dataside manner" may amuse you. It conjures up the image of a smooth-talking hustler reassuring suckers that their data will yield astounding results, if only they will pay the consultant high fees for a numbers massage. Or the image may anger you, as it does many statisticians. Every statistician knows that many clients are ignorant of what statistics is and are easy marks for the statistician hustler. As a matter of fact, most statisticians *hate* charlatans, particularly charlatans of the science world. They are thus very suspicious that the statistician who has charm will use it for evil, covering up bad science by soothing bad scientists and getting rich in the bargain.

Here are three cases that illustrate how emotions affect the success of a consulting session. It was near the end of the first hour of consultation between George Williams, a statistical consultant who had recently joined the organization, and Mr. Winslow, a fellow employee whom George had met for the first time that day. As the session was ending and they were beginning to discuss who was going to do what work before the next session, Mr. Winslow said that he was planning to show the statistical recommendations to his boss and to two other friends in his division of the company. He also said that his permanent position was in New Orleans, and upon returning there, he would ask a colleague who knew something about statistics whether George's recommendations were reasonable. Mr. Winslow questioned whether a complicated or a relatively straightforward statistical analysis should be used in this situation.

Upon hearing Mr. Winslow's plans to get another statistical opinion, George become upset and terminated the consulting session quickly. During the next three weeks, George investigated the question of which analysis was appropriate for the data; he had assumed this was his job. After George had spent approximately ten hours on his investigation, Mr. Winslow called long distance and informed George that he had decided to use the simple analysis on the problem and that he was looking forward to getting together with George to discuss subsequent parts of the problem. George became angry, having wasted ten hours on work in which Mr. Winslow was not at all interested. George was not looking forward to the next consulting session. He began to think of ways of avoiding Mr. Winslow.

Karen Marrow is a Ph.D. sociologist in the marketing division of a company. Bryan James is a statistical consultant in the research group that works with the chemists and biologists involved with product development. Dr. Marrow recognized that she had a statistical problem beyond her level of expertise and decided to call Mr. James to arrange for a consulting appointment. The Marrow and James families occasionally socialize together. Bryan told Dr. Marrow that he is training an apprentice consultant who will also be at the session. Later, on her way to the consulting session, Karen realized that she was feeling uneasy. She was not confident of her statistical knowledge and the thought of having her ignorance exposed to a statistician and his apprentice was unsettling to her, even though she knows Bryan.

During the session, Bryan wasted no time getting to the heart of the statistical issue that Karen brought in. Frequently in the session he raised questions relating to the type of data available, the level of measurement, the quality of the random sampling, and the response rate. As each issue arose in turn, his questions elicited from Karen repeated apologies for the quality of the data, such as, "We sociologists have to deal with lots of very soft data. We don't get as good data as you scientists get." On hearing these apologies, Bryan felt uncomfortable but proceeded to ask additional technical questions. By the close of the session, some of Karen's statistical issues had been answered. She left, however, feeling uncomfortable about the whole activity and wondering whether the solutions she had received were worth the price she had paid in embarrassment. She hoped to avoid statisticians in the future.

Tom Jaret is a statistical consultant who has been with the company for one year since he finished his master's degree in statistics. Jeanne Bailey is a senior researcher in genetics who has worked in the lab for about fifteen years. At the beginning of their first session, Dr. Bailey asked, "Mr. Jaret, are you new at the company? Do you have your Ph.D. in statistics?" Tom, quietly seething at the suggestion that he might not have enough expertise because of having only a master's degree, answered, "I have been here for a year. I only have my master's degree in statistics." The session began and Dr. Bailey described in great length the series of genetics experiments she and her co-workers have been doing for the last five years. It was clear that this work was her pride and joy. Gradually, she got closer and closer to the question that brought her to the consultant today, namely, how to analyze some data for a paper to be presented in two months. Dr. Bailey had done some preliminary regression analyses. When Tom inquired as to how these regressions have been done, Dr. Bailey described how she had used her desk calculator to do them. Tom was surprised to learn that a senior scientist approached data analysis in this old-fashioned way. Tom then was relieved to be able to give his client some advice. He gleefully exclaimed, "There are lots of easier ways of doing regression analyses than that! You should get this data onto a computer file and use the computer programs that will do this very fast and very easily!"

Dr. Bailey, instead of feeling grateful for the advice, felt foolish. She began to explain that no one in her area uses computers, that it was not something she had seen in graduate school, and that it is just not a technology she was very familiar with. Tom then realized that tension was building, and tried to put Dr. Bailey at ease by describing his own early experiences with large computers and how they had intimidated him. He said that he appreciated Dr. Bailey's aversion to large computers. He then offered to explain some painless ways of learning about them. The tension eased. They both then discussed how the analyses could be done and what analyses would be appropriate.

COMMUNICATION

Nonverbal Communication

Office Arrangement.   The physical surroundings of the meeting place for your consultation have an effect. How much effect they have on different people varies, but they have some effect on everyone. To the extent you can control the physical surroundings of your consultations, you can influence your mood and that of your clients. In particular, if you want to put a frightened client more at ease, it is good to start with the right physical setting.

There is one overwhelming advantage to planning an atmosphere of friendliness in the physical sense. The statistician with low social skills who is tense and self-conscious with people can plan the physical setting while still alone. If the place of consultation is your office, you need to be able to have at least one "friendly" furniture arrangement.

To understand office arrangements and the moods they suggest, picture yourself meeting the president of the United States. In this setting, you are aware of several factors, all influencing your desire to be open and cooperative. One of them is whether you meet at your place or his. Maybe your office is more convenient than his, but there is an implication that the host is more important. You are traveling to the president's office partly because his time is more valuable than yours, and traveling time is not productive. In general, the meeting in an office is a psychological advantage to the host. It is his or her territory. There are other reasons for choosing the meeting site, of course. Sometimes I ask not to meet in my office simply because I want to see somebody else's place or just want to get away from the phone or want a break from routine. Still, *where* you meet has implications for status, and the meeting is usually at the office of the person granting the favor or the person of higher status.

The next step in exploring your feelings as you enter the Oval Office is to picture two different situations. In one, the president is sitting behind his desk and the obvious chair for you is in front. The desk is between you. In the second, he has a small table off to the side of his desk, with two comfortable chairs by it and coffee cups, cream, sugar, and pot on the table. As you enter, he moves toward the table with apparent intent for you to join him there.

Because you are dealing with the president and nothing with him is simple, you are still on guard in the second setting. For whatever reason, though, in the second setting he wants a less hurried interchange and the two identical comfortable chairs connote a momentary equality. Imagine how you would feel if you entered the Oval Office and saw no chairs other than the president's. The implication would be that you would *stand* during the meeting, helping to make it short.

If a client meets you in your office and you want to make the physical surroundings friendly, have an arrangement of equal chairs. By all means, do not have your desk between you and your frightened clients. Having your desk between you and your visitor is good for establishing formal distance, something you may want if you have to fire a subordinate.

Another thing you notice about the Oval Office is that it says he is the president. Similarly, your office can say you are a statistician. All it takes is enough books with statistics covers and a calculating device. The office can say that you are an expert. The way you *arrange* the office will say whether you are formal or informal.

Clothes, Body Language, and Eye Contact.   The arrangement of your office for your meetings with frightened clients is only one aspect of nonverbal communication. There are obviously many other aspects, including dress, appearance, and body language. The nice aspect of office arrangement is that you can think it through in private without the confusing stimulus of the presence of a client. The same is true of dress. You can decide by yourself what to wear that day. The other nonverbals, however, such as physical appearance, body language, and facial expression, are very difficult to change. There is bad news and good news in this for you. The bad news is that you would have a very difficult time altering them to put your frightened clients at ease. The good news is that they are more reliable indicators of how people feel, and you can learn to read these signs to see how your clients are feeling. If their words and body language (facial expressions) don't match, chances are the nonverbals more accurately reflect their true feelings. It is easy to learn to lie about one's feelings with words, but difficult with nonverbals; they're much harder to control.

Envision a television screen behind your head. Suppose you are asking the "right questions," but in your mind you are asking yourself questions like, "How can anyone be interested in this? This is truly a trivial area. I think that this client doesn't appreciate the first part of experimental design. I wonder what I should have for supper tonight." Suppose that the television screen behind your head is not projecting the words that come out of your mouth, but the thoughts going on in your brain. Certainly, if this were to happen, you would try hard to edit or control these thoughts.

Although there is not a television set behind your head, your nonverbal communication, namely, what you do with your face, your body, your tone of voice, and your eyes, is a highly accurate indicator of what kinds of thoughts are going through your head. If you are bored, your nonverbal communication will probably indicate that. Think about how your client might feel reading that message on the "television set" behind your head. If you are going to spend the time consulting with this client, it is best to invest yourself as much and as genuinely as possible and put your whole brain to work on the project. If you are bored, clients will spot it. If you can't make yourself concentrate, reassure clients that their problem is important but that you are too tired or worried about something else. Admit to yourself what is happening to you. Apologize and reschedule the meeting. Sometimes coffee works for me, but other times I just get hyper on it without being able to think better.

There is an implicit message here: *Keep an eye on your client.* We don't mean a hypnotic stare, but reasonably frequent glancing. Looking at the client from time to time is unnatural for many statisticians. For one thing, it is tempting to get totally absorbed in the intellectual task of the problem. For another, many statisticians would rather not "play psychologist." Statisticians tend to be task-oriented rather than people-oriented and prefer looking at data on pieces of paper while talking rather than keeping an eye on the client. Looking at paper while talking cuts you off from monitoring the client's feelings. The client, being polite, doesn't talk while you do, and you can't see the client's face if your eyes are glued to the data. Ruling out touch, taste, and smell in the typical consultation, your not looking at your clients while you talk is the best way to ignore their fear.

Open Verbal Communication

Clients typically resent that statisticians have power over them. They intimidate clients because clients don't understand statisticians' rules, which clients must nevertheless obey. Statisticians make clients feel dumb and put down. Your job is to prove that *you* are not that way; you cannot prove to clients that *statisticians* are not that way. This distinction is a fine one and will test your ability to resist temptation to defend your field and your colleagues. Remember that you do not have to *agree* with clients; you need only to acknowledge and accept their feelings. It helps for you to add that statistics *does* have an image problem (it does) and that many people feel the way your client does. One of the statistics image jokes may release some of the tension.

Encourage your clients to think and talk plans through

with you. Control your own impatience if they aren't very good at it. Make sure you don't subtly scold or put them down. One way you can help clients is by simply sitting silently while they are thinking quietly or even out loud. Similarly, there are times when you need just to sit silently and think about your plans for statistical recommendations. This suggestion may seem oversimplistic, but it's common to feel uncomfortable when a conversation lapses into silence. Some silence is golden in two-person problem solving. It enables you to focus on the problem you are considering, rather than having to think simultaneously about the problem *and* process the verbal input coming from the other person. You may need to explain to the client that this is what is going on when you are being silent and that you can't process more information at the moment. It is important that clients believe you are not playing a game with them. Reassure them that your only interest in talking over all your proposals is in making sure there is clear communication between you and the client relative to the problem. This discussion will enable you to learn how much of your proposal has been comprehended. It also gives clients a chance to check out their perception of the proposal and whether or not they can verbalize what is to be done.

FEAR

Mike, a senior statistician at a large corporation, is very conscientious. His clientele consists of a dozen scientists with whom he has worked for several years. They all know each other well. Although he thinks they are good scientists, they do something that drives him crazy. They leave him out of their meetings when they design their studies. He has told them repeatedly how important it is for a statistician to be involved from the beginning. He finally got them to send him announcements of their design meetings, but the announcements arrived too late. It bothered Mike enough that he called a meeting to discuss the problem. After a couple of hours of awkward dancing around to avoid hurt feelings, he concluded that his clients see him as too critical a person.

They stated clearly, with apparent honesty, that they greatly respect his ability and conscientiousness, but implied he is too rigid to help them with the free-wheeling planning session. He gathered from the meeting that they see him as a "heavy" and felt any shortcuts they choose to take regarding scientific rigor had best be done without his knowledge.

Mike's story illustrates one of the great frustrations of a statistical consultant. By being very up-front with high scientific and ethical standards, a statistician frightens away clients who feel they can't measure up in those areas. Among such clients are those who are *forced* to see a statistician and are cautious about revealing embarrassing compromises of quality.

Many clients lack personal self-confidence and job security. They are afraid. Their study is not going well and they're afraid of being fired. They feel personally inadequate and intimidated by statistics. Evidence of their dread is the gossip in the hallways about the pain of working with statisticians. Another symptom is observed in the clients' discomfort during consultation—the apologies and nervousness. The real impact of their fear is seen in another subtle, but important way: at the third or seventh meeting, they reveal material you wanted to know at the first meeting, but the clients had to build up their courage to tell you embarrassing facts. This has happened to us many times.

The essence of our recommendation is that you consider the problem of client fear important and devote energy to solving it. Some statisticians harbor the illusion that interactions between scientists and statisticians are intellectual but not emotional. As a result, they set aside their natural skills in diagnosing client fear and try to act as though it doesn't matter.

There are a couple of reasons statisticians tend to ignore client fear. The first is that they can diagnose it but are ill at ease in treating it. They're not sure what to do and would rather not do psychology. The second reason is that the beginning statistician is afraid and hopes to receive comfort rather than give it. Of what are statisticians afraid? Making mistakes and looking foolish. They want to see themselves as bright and knowledgeable and be seen that way by others.

They are under heavy performance pressure and afraid of failing. Being afraid, they have diminished powers of observation of the client's fear. Thus, our suggesting that you devote mental energy to diagnosing and treating client fear is suggesting you take some concentration away from science and statistics. We do strongly suggest it, however, asserting that it will pay off in the long run.

There is more than one way to treat client fear. Treatments need to be tailored to you and to the client. It is an art, not a science; no two people practice it identically. Though it is an art, it can be learned. The most primitive method of treating client fear is projecting, that is, presume the client feels like you do and is basically the same kind of person. This is simply the Golden Rule, "Do unto others what you would have them do unto you." In this model, you presume the client feels the way you would were you in his or her situation and act accordingly. This strategy is definitely better than ignoring the problem of client fear, but it is only a first approximation. It is less effective than considering the client to be a unique individual, perhaps quite unlike you. As a start, there are some good bets as to what *might* be making the client afraid.

Causes of Client Fear

The client's career is at stake with the study and he is afraid you will find fatal flaws in it that he doesn't know about. He thinks you have the power to pronounce his work invalid. This fear can exist even presuming you have no ill will toward him or his work. It is the same as the fear of going to a psychiatrist who without malice, could have you committed to an insane asylum.

He fears that you are a negative person and will use your knowledge to discredit his work on mere technicalities. His fear of you as a negative person is that you will ridicule him privately and publicly.

She is ashamed of her lack of statistical knowledge and blames herself for not knowing how to do it herself. She fears that you will explicitly or implicitly scold her in this tender area.

To appreciate your clients' fears and their impact on their behavior, it is sobering to list your own fears. If you discover some in yourself, you will at least be more sympathetic to your clients' fears. You may also see how they can, unchecked, distort your interaction.

Common Consultant Fears

Consultants may fear they will look inadequate to their clients by not having an "answer" or seeming slow to understand the study. They may also fear that their response to the client will be judged inadequate by the statistical community because it is at too low a level or not thorough enough.

Consequences of Fear

There is a problem caused by either the consultant or client being afraid: The frightened person is more self-centered and less able to think about the needs of others. Frightened statisticians need to protect themselves more than help the client. When both the client and the statistician are frightened, each tends to increase the other's fear or anger. Statisticians who are afraid they will not impress the client with their speed in grasping the problem tend to interrupt the client's explanation in order to show what quick thinkers they are. Clients who feel defensive about not knowing enough statistics tend to interpret the statistician's interruptions as impatience with a slow-witted client. These clients then tend to keep quiet about anything they're unsure of, leading the statistician to safe, but perhaps minor, corners of the study. The misunderstanding here is that both statisticians and clients are afraid of not impressing each other with their intelligence. It is reassuring for the helper to impress the helpee with his or her competence, but it is destructive to *compete* with the helpee.

Statisticians who are afraid that their work is too low level to impress the statistical community tend to use techniques neither the client nor the client's audience has ever heard of. *Sometimes* it is necessary to use techniques new to clients and their audience, but they worry the client who wants to be in complete intellectual charge of this study (an admirable trait).

Eliminating Fears

What can a statistician do about a frightened client who withholds for fear of being embarrassed or scolded? Stated this way, the answer seems obvious. Why not *order* the client to "tell me everything and don't be embarrassed or be afraid of being scolded"? The problem is that telling someone how to feel doesn't work. That is, they don't feel the way you tell them to, and particularly not right away. It doesn't work to say to the depressed person, "Cheer up. It's Christmas"; to the panicky mother, "Don't worry, we're doing everything we can to find your daughter"; or to the irate husband, "You should be glad your mother-in-law wants to live with you." For one person to control another's mood takes great skill. To get a frightened client to relax and cooperate fully requires creating an atmosphere of trust and patience.

Controlling Your Fears.   The first step is for consultants to control their own fears as best they can and devote some energy to relaxing the client. We recognize that devoting energy to the care and comfort of the frightened client does detract from concentrating on the scientific and statistical problems, but we continue to claim that it is cost-effective in the long run.

Probing the Client's Fears.   The second step is by casual conversation, to probe politely for areas of fear in the client. In probing for the fear that you have the power to pronounce the study invalid, say something like, "A lot of people who come to statisticians overestimate the authority we have. They believe the myth that there's only one right way to analyze data. Actually, there often are several good ways and statisticians do disagree with each other." If the client is intimidated by your authority to denounce his or her study, these remarks will visibly help.

If the client fears that statisticians are too negative and like to put clients down, a remark like, "One of the problems statisticians have is our public image as fussy nitpickers. There's some truth in that image, but a lot of us are trying hard to change" will evoke a positive response. If the client is embarrassed that she's not a good enough statistician herself, try saying, "I admire people who try to be their own statisticians, but I think they're expecting too much of themselves. I had to study statistics for years before I learned what it is all about. I certainly couldn't handle an additional field myself."

Comforting Clients.   Everyone has a little natural skill at comforting frightened people; some have a great deal of such skill and thus tend to do well in nurturing jobs. Most people by instinct want to comfort a frightened child or crying kitten. The skills here are simple and instinctive, with much holding and simple comforting talk. It is easy to comfort children or kittens because they are nonthreatening to you. Thus, if you have the time and feel in the mood, you will probably do it well.

Suppose, however, that the frightened child is your own. She has kept you up for four nights with crying and nightmares, and you're getting very short on sleep. You pace and carry on and say soothing words, but it crosses your mind that if you were less mature, or drunk, you might neglect or even try spanking the child. You are still intolerant of child beaters but entertain the possibility that they need help rather than a prison sentence. In other words, knowing how to comfort is one thing, but having the wrong circumstances can make it quite difficult. You don't love your clients like you do your child. The setting is very different. You can be having a bad day, be worried about handling the problem well technically, or even be annoyed by the client. The trick is to be able to comfort others even when you don't feel like it, and *that* is what takes the practice.

One good thing is that you don't have to practice on clients; you can practice on anybody. A good time for practice is any time you are feeling hassled and with someone who is feeling frightened and inadequate and seeking reassurance. Getting better at this means you can do it in situations in which you feel less inclined. Remember the cardinal rule:

Don't *tell* people not to be afraid. Give them facts (that they will believe) that will help. It is often effective to express your perception of their fear. For example, if a client is afraid of being scolded by his boss because his experiment failed to produce the result the company wants, you can't tell him the boss won't be angry. You can tell him, though, that you've been in similar situations and that you respect him (if you do) for his integrity. You can add that you appreciate the burden of a scientist having to work for an employer with unscientific goals.

Building the Base.   Think hard about the introductory part of the session. In this phase, the two individuals begin to get to know each other. Ideally, they begin to build a trusting, open relationship. If you are known in the company, the client's sizing you up will be partly based on your reputation. If you are new to the company, part of the client's image of you will depend on how your predecessors did their job. It is useful to you to find out who these predecessors were and how they related to their clients. What did the clients think of them? A young consultant in a drug industry statistical group noted that she was having difficulty establishing consulting relationships with some of the scientists in the research group. She later learned that the scientists had a bad experience with the previous statistical consultant who had been in her job. Client memories of these experiences die slowly.

Try making the introductory part of your statistical consulting sessions more productive. Get a picture of your client as a person, perhaps by discussing his or her professional background. Many consultants rush this part of the session. With a new client who is scheduled for an hour-long appointment, it is reasonable to spend ten minutes in introductory activity. You will know if clients want to move from introductory activities into the problem by their pulling you out of a general conversation into specific questions relating to their problem. You also may feel restless if it is too long. If so, *ask* if the client wants to get into the problem rather than assuming he or she does.

In the introduction, you will unconsciously communicate to the client whether you want to have a relaxed or rushed schedule for the meeting. Some clients want to "explore" your office before settling down to business. Others are restless until they are offered coffee. Beginning an immediate interrogation of clients in a new room means that your questions may compete with their desire to familiarize themselves visually with your office. If they seem to want it, give them time to do it. Keep in mind that they are in your territory.

We have noticed that nervous young statistical consultants tend to rush the introductory activities. The young statistical consultant tends to underestimate the importance of social comfort in consulting. A rush to the statistical material may undermine the development of a relaxed learning environment and the creation of trust between the two individuals. If the client's prior experience with statisticians has been negative, the impatient introduction may well reinforce those negative impressions.

Creating the Best Setting.   Think about the settings most conducive to learning. What are the characteristics of this environment? It is one in which you are not intimidated by the other person. There is a minimum of distractions interfering with the learning. The atmosphere is relaxed; the physical surroundings are comfortable. You are both patient with each other, taking the time to provide ample preparations and motivation for why the other should learn the material that you have to teach. You each encourage the other to be an active participant in the session. Material that is taught is clearly demonstrated relative to how it can be used. Where possible, you practice doing a calculation or two. The atmosphere is characterized by substantial amounts of encouragement. When it is your turn, you listen to the material that the client is sharing with you. You don't interrupt the flow of information with your eagerness to show how much you know about what the client is teaching you. There is no competition for the floor; it is not a contest to see who can talk the most and the fastest.

ANGER

Anger is distinctly different from fear. Fear leads to anger, and anger leads to fight. Although there is much more fear than anger in statistical clients and some fear looks superficially like anger, genuine anger does occur. It is destructive to the consultation in a different way than fear is. A client who is forced to see you may well be angry. You can be angry at a client who appears to enjoy making your job more difficult by being noncooperative.

Sources of Anger

Clients can be angry at statisticians for nit-picking a study to death and never seeming satisfied with anything clients do. There are clients who have been terminally abraded by an arrogant statistician and henceforth seek statistical help as cheerfully as they go to the dentist.

Dealing with anger is different from dealing with fear. It is harder to defuse anger than to comfort a frightened person, especially where you are trying to lessen the anger of someone who is angry at *you*. There are clients who are angry at statisticians in general, seeing them as roadblocks to progress. There are also statisticians who are angry at all clients who bring messy problems that make a statistician's life too difficult.

Much of the anger seen in clients is due to their being *forced* to consult with statisticians. Clients are forced by journal editors and corporate or governmental rules. In one pharmaceutical company, all research proposals must be signed by the statistical unit. When the rule was instituted, all the statisticians, including the department head, were young, barely over thirty years of age. The older senior scientists were furious at the new company rule and made their discontent very clear to the statisticians. The statisticians reminded the scientists that the statistical unit didn't institute the rule, but that didn't help much. For one thing, the senior scientists are battle-wise in company politics and know too well the infighting among departments. When a department's power is increased overnight by an order from the top, the favored department is never above suspicion for backroom maneuvering. Thus, the statisticians couldn't be totally convincing that they had had nothing to do with their sudden increase in authority. They have gotten somewhat used to it, but it still is annoying and the digs and barbs still occur. It gets in the way of cooperation, with some scientists trying to slip things by the statisticians. What can statisticians do in this kind of situation?

Defusing Anger

The essence of defusing the expression of anger is not to argue with it, but accept it. No matter what the anger is, you can substantially diminish it by letting that person know (1) you are not trying to talk him out of it, (2) you just want to understand it, and (3) you are going to accept it and agree that his being angry makes sense, from his point of view. Notice that this is exactly what two people verbally fighting with each other do not do. They are absolutely self-centered during the argument and think only of ways to hurt the other person, including blaming him or her for starting the argument.

Defusing a client's anger is more difficult than reassuring a frightened one. You can practice on all kinds of people. In your daily encounters with people all the way from loved ones to clerks in stores, there are people anxious to have their anger understood and accepted by anyone who will take time to do it. Politicians exploit this as best they can, but they go one step further. They make voters think that the candidate has not only heard their frustrations, but that the candidate will make every effort to remedy the situation. We do not recommend that you promise to eliminate every client irritation, but only to hear it.

Anger at Statisticians.   The effectiveness of defusing the expression of anger by understanding it and accepting it is often very dramatic. If clients are forced to come to you, even if they don't show dramatic outward signs of anger, it works well to say, "If I were in your shoes, I think I'd be too upset to come and see me. I might just read the riot act to the person who made me do it." This, or an equivalent, invites clients to open up about the forcing process. If they do, listen attentively and with acceptance as they describe how they were pushed into coming to see you. If they repeat themselves, it's because they think you haven't heard them; so acknowledge their specific points, not by a general statement such as "I hear you," but by a specific statement such as, "I can see why a researcher of your experience would be furious." This latter statement would be a great comment if the clients' anger is due to their feeling an insult to their status. Keep a sharp eye out for anger in clients regarding status insult. It is common. To appreciate its impact on clients, recall how you felt the last time you heard someone insult the status of statisticians.

If clients are angry and pick up on your offer to talk about it, encourage them to cover the main points. The benefit to science is that your understanding their anger, accepting that they have it, and agreeing that it makes sense from their point of view encourages them to be open with you about study weaknesses. It helps clients trust you if they see you as a generally understanding person. Understanding and accepting clients' anger does not mean you have to *agree* with them. You don't need to lie.

Generalized Anger.   There are other things clients are angry at, such as having had a bad day. A statement to the apparently angry client such as "I'm concentrating pretty well today. Sometimes I'm so worked up over other things, my consulting is useless" will make you seem more human and invite clients to unburden themselves regarding the fact that they're still preoccupied with other irritations.

Anger at You.   The hardest cases to handle are those in which the client is angry at you. It's difficult not to get dragged into a verbal fight. The last time I recall a client being openly hostile to me was over his bill. He and I had worked together previously on something for which I didn't charge him because his work was of special benefit to me professionally, but he knew that I charge most clients for service. The most recent time we worked together, however, I saw it as service but failed to communicate that at the outset. When I brought up the topic of the bill at the end, he was very annoyed. He had assumed that our relationship would *always* be collegial and his having to pay was insulting. I thus felt angry and defensive. Hiding my own hostility from him (I think), I went on to apologize excessively about not being clearer at the beginning of *this* consultation. I then sounded very defensive about the policy of charging clients, and I went on to explain the distinction between what is routine for me and what is professionally advantageous. It was a partial success.

Expressing Anger

Remember that statistical clients are not likely to yell or break furniture. They are more likely to have a seething resentment of what they think statistics and statisticians are doing to them. They think statisticians get in their way, forcing them to use methods they can't understand and don't like. Statistics infringes upon their freedom to conclude what they wish as they observe data. There are more than a few clients who have learned that statistical significance and practical significance have nothing to do with each other and conclude that statistical tests are a conspiracy to create jobs for statisticians. They don't see that we statisticians have no power to impose our thought processes on the world, but powerful nonstatisticians who believe in statistics do the imposing. There are scientists out there who beat up other scientists, using us as the weapon. We shouldn't be surprised that the victim resents the weapon.

The expression of this anger is sometimes an isolated bitter remark, but it's usually a heel-dragging reluctance to cooperate, to open up and talk freely about the study. Refusal to let you in on the plans or visit the lab can be consequences of client anger. You can offer to visit the lab, but you have to be invited. This requires a hospitable, not hostile, client.

SUMMARY

• Client fear of statistics and statisticians is the biggest consulting problem. It makes clients withhold key information and cooperation.

• Perfectionism and fear of technical inadequacy makes statisticians appear intimidating.

• When in doubt as to what your clients are feeling, reassure and comfort them. Tell them how you are perceiving them and check the accuracy of your perceptions.

• Accept your client's feelings about statistics, statisticians in general, and you in particular. Never *tell* clients how to feel.

• Taking care of your client psychologically and socially when you're threatened yourself is hard work, but it pays off.

CHAPTER 10

The Statistician on a Research Team

In the previous chapters, we have considered the statistician in a one-to-one relationship with a client. Sometimes the client brings along some assistants (laboratory technicians, perhaps), but it is still clear that your relationship is with one person and the assistants are there to answer questions of detail or observe. They are not deciders on major policy issues. We already treated the complexities encountered when the person you're talking to is a messenger and you cannot talk to the client.

In this chapter, we consider the problems of n people on a research team that includes you, with no one of the other $n-1$ being designated as the client. They have different areas of expertise and different roles to play on the team, but all have decision-making authority. The interactions on a research team can be very complex, with the addition or deletion of a key person making a world of difference in how a group interacts. As an analogy to the complexities of adding one more person, we note that physicists have solved the problem of predicting the paths of two physical objects, each with its own mass and velocity and interacting only with each other. They have not, however, solved the corresponding problem with three physical objects.

Another illustration of rapidly increasing complexity is the creation of families by adoption agencies. The couple who has only one child and that child is adopted thinks that the adoption agency should be eager to place another child with them because they have proved they can successfully handle adopted children. The adoption agency, on the other hand, knows that placing another child with that couple is trying to construct a workable *four*-person group, whereas in placing the first child they are constructing a workable *three*-person group, which is much easier.

UNDERSTANDING GROUP DYNAMICS

Statisticians on research teams consisting of at least two deciding members other than the statistician are frequently frustrated because the group moves so slowly, goes off on tangents, bogs down, and is ridden with interpersonal tension. These problems frustrate the statisticians, who want to get on with science and statistics. Showing impatience to the group in the wrong way or at the wrong time will cause the group to exclude statisticians more rather than include them more. They will then see their influence diminishing and lose their cool, making their exclusion worse. All they will be left with in the end is their righteous indignation while the rest of the group confirms their prejudice that statisticians don't work well with people.

The reason that some research groups move so slowly and awkwardly, in the eyes of statisticians, is that the group members have personal social needs they must meet before they will cooperate fully with the group's primary task. In other words, the "noise" of statistical consulting, the people problem, is even louder on research teams than it is with one-to-one consulting, and more complicated. It is worthwhile for a statistician to understand the group dynamics of research teams in order to gain more influence.

I was asked by Bill, a competent researcher, to join a group of investigators he was pulling together for the purpose of designing a study he had been thinking about for several years. He had never done a project of the magnitude he was proposing, but is a very confident man who had no doubts we could do it. He told me he planned to ask Tess, Ralph, and Diane to join the group. Each one was to bring a different strength to the team. Tess is very good researcher on small projects. She loves detail work and is very conscientious. Neither Ralph nor Diane is good at the concepts of research, but Ralph has a senior position relative to Bill and would be a political asset to have. Ralph also knows a little about research. Diane was brought in because she was very enthusiastic about the project and had control of the materials essential to it. Diane is very weak in research methodology, but a particularly nice and cooperative person. The group's first goal was to convince the federal government to fund the project, which was extremely expensive.

Bill told me confidentially his purposes in bringing in Tess and Diane and that he was planning to keep Diane in the "backroom" when we got to the point of being cross-examined by the funders. Bill feared that Diane would get the research plan mixed up in her mind and thus give the funders the impression that the team is generally ignorant about research methodology. Diane would be counted on to do her part of the project very conscientiously. Bill was a little worried about Tess also, but Tess had a generally good presence in cross-examinations. Ralph was destined to play a minor role and stick to a narrow corner.

I agreed with Bill's assessment of the other team members, but worried that his plan was too grandiose and we were asking for too much money. Bill told me to relax, that there would be "no problem." "They'll have to give it to us," he said. I don't know what confidential conversations Bill had with the other members, but I suppose that he did have some. Bill is a very political animal and always seems to be compaigning for a higher position in the organization.

With all this going on in the background, you can see that our meetings had some hidden agendas. Bill, the acknowledged team leader, was trying to make Diane feel important in spite of her irrelevant comments about the research design. Tess held forth quite a bit, but couldn't add to the research design either. They all seemed to defer to me on the design, but I knew the sample size was too small for the variability of responses and the multiple inference problem of too many observations on too few subjects. We went around and around on this point. They listened attentively while I talked, but I didn't convince them. I dropped it but warned them that I couldn't cover it up if the funders spotted it.

The funders met with all of us once for two days. They clobbered us. They picked up on Tess's and Diane's misunderstanding of the design and the divergence of my views from theirs. Because Tess and Diane would do major parts of the study, the funders had no faith in it. Bill tried to smooth things over and make it seem as though what I was saying was compatible with Tess's and Diane's views, but it was useless. I'm sure the funders saw through it and probably thought Bill had a problem with logic. (Bill did understand, though.) The funders put me on the stand and asked me if I thought we agreed with each other. I said no. Bill cringed noticeably.

We tried an appeal a couple of months later, with just Bill, Tess, and me facing a different group of about ten examiners. We had a much more coherent presentation but still lost. Bill's interpretation was that we had a good study planned and that our rejection was on political rather than scientific grounds. I thought justice was done, frankly, and that we shouldn't have gotten funding. The sample size just wasn't big enough, even if everything else went well.

What is the lesson of this experience? Outside of the sample size problem, there were dominant social agendas in the group. Tess was politically important to Bill, and Diane wasn't going to do her share of the work on the project unless she had the status of a co-investigator. The whole plan failed.

You may well respond by saying that research teams shouldn't have agendas other than the pursuit of scientific truth. Well, some do, and statisticians can't eliminate those other agendas. Our job is to learn how to be effective in the face of them. The most natural mistake for statisticians to make in a study group is to be too impatient with the social processes. They take time and they're important to group members. As frustrating as it is, even statisticians and scientists who are as dedicated to the pursuit of truth as any human can be are still human and have status needs. Many of the "dedicated" ones have all their ego eggs in the one basket called their career. They are very sensitive to remarks that have evaluative overtones about their work because it reflects so much on them as persons.

Many research groups do not have good leaders who know how to manage people. These groups are chaotic and behave like a family with too many children competing for the limited attention of harried parents. Group members whose egos are bruised put their energy into gaining group respect, and their participation is slanted toward that goal. If two members are competing for the leadership role, their struggle will take up much group time.

Overtalkative Members

One of the problems to notice in a research team is members who talk too much, demanding way too much group time. The compulsive talkers may repeat themselves over and over again or keep contributing wild ideas that can't possibly work. A competent group leader will guess that talkative members feel insecure about their status in the group and thus give recognition to them, hoping they will feel reassured and talk less. The highly competent group leader, to control overtalkative members who keep repeating the same point, will repeat the point to make sure the member knows that at least the leader got the message. If the leader says only, "I've got your point, Ted," Ted is still not sure what point the leader has. If nobody in the group re-

peats Ted's message in Ted's own words, he will keep sending it in various forms until he's sure someone understands
it. He may even repeat it until someone of high status in the
group *thanks* him for the idea.

If no one else in the group recognizes Ted's suggestion,
you should repeat it back to Ted in (almost) his own words.
If you consider it a contribution, say something to the effect
that his point is helpful. The other group members will be
glad you stopped Ted's repetition, and Ted will be grateful to
you for the recognition. This gesture will increase your prestige in the group and cause the other members to listen with
more credence to your statistical points. The gesture will also
weaken the stereotype of you as a narrow statistician, and
other group members will think you are a good team player.

Negative Stereotypes

It is common for a statistician on a research team to
hear in the remarks of the other members the usual negative
stereotypes of statisticians. You'll get a better long-range result in the group if you can appear to take them as light-
hearted, good-natured teasing and not appear defensive. The
main stereotype to counteract is that you are interested only
in your own narrow view of the project and are disinterested in what anyone has to say if it doesn't involve your
area. The best thing you can do in a research group is be
interested in the big picture and keep the statistics in perspective. Don't convey that you think the statistics issues are always the most important on the project by acting
disinterested in the other areas.

Statistician's Role

There is another key tactic to your being influential in
the group. Definitely do not convey, particularly in a condescending manner, that your role in the group is to keep the
rest of them honest. Statisticians frequently hear from other
statisticians, as well as nonstatisticians, that one of their roles
is to keep other people honest. There is some truth in it, but it
is very irritating because it connotes a moral-ethical superi-

ority. The group will not cooperate with you if they think you are suspicious of them. They will fully cooperate with you only if they think of you as a team member sharing the team goals, not as a local sheriff ready to turn them in.

This may in fact put you in an ethical bind, but you can impose a statistician's conscience into the group values without the group rejecting you personally. Just say that if they do the study in the manner that you consider unethical, there is a danger that some other statistician might catch the mistake and you could not defend it without losing your reputation in the statistical community. If the group continues to push, say, without sarcastic or pouty tones, that they may be able to find another statistician who could support their plan. They will probably not even look for another statistician. To make the threat without having the group reject you, it is vital that you not seem morally superior to them, but simply afraid for your own reputation as a statistician. Convey your spirit of wanting to get the job done, but that this design won't do it.

Loyalty

You will also increase your influence on a research team by conveying a project-team loyalty rather than a loyalty to the field of statistics. *Loyalty* to statistics is different from *competence* in statistics. They certainly want you to be competent in statistics.

Individual Versus Group Behavior

Another technique for building your influence in the group is to get to know the group members through one-to-one conversations. One of the dramatic group phenomena is the very different personalities people exhibit in one-to-one conversations versus in a group. Be prepared to find some of them very different people when you are alone with them. Be prepared to find that you get a very different impression of what they want from the group and are prepared to give to it, compared to the impression you get of their personal goals when you hear them in the group.

In the healthy, effective research team, there is less discrepancy between group behavior and individual behavior, but in the troubled group there are great discrepancies. This phenomenon is as much due to the group as it is due to the individual. To appreciate this last point, notice how differently people behave when they are with their parents, children, spouse, or colleagues. The presence or absence of powerful authority figures matters enormously in group behavior. After getting to know better from one-to-one conversations what each member wants and plans to give, you will be more effective in the group. Your making the effort to give your individual attention to their views will encourage them to listen to your views. The solid one-to-one conversations will improve your influence in the group as much as anything you do in the meetings of the whole group. Remember that you must have influence unless you want to be relegated to the narrow position the group assigns to you. The narrow position commonly assigned to the statistician in a research group is that of data analyst, when in fact the statistician should be invited to comment on design and general research logic.

Advancing Within the Group

Opportunities for advancement in a group are most apt to arise in the chaotic group with shaky leadership. One research team I was on is a good example of the chaotic group. The main reason for this chaos was the fact that there were two co-principal investigators of equal status whose styles of work clashed. Randy is very impatient and wanted to avoid going off on tangents to make sure we met the deadline and didn't overspend the budget. Steve is just the opposite. He is a perfectionist who loves details and going off on every interesting tangent. Steve has a hard time making a decision and wants very much to be well liked.

The clash between the work styles of Randy and Steve consumed the weekly meetings in the first few weeks of the project. The clash was only about work style, as the two got along well socially. Several substantive experts came in periodically from all parts of the country. They comprised the project advisory board. They weren't getting paid much, and were doing it for the prestige of being co-authors on the report.

Steve wanted to be liked and respected by the members of the advisory board, several of whom had higher status than Steve and could do him some good. Every time advisory board members wanted something done their way, Steve tried to placate them and promised we would do it somewhat that way. Randy grew more and more impatient with Steve and saw his promises as unrealistic and ruinous to the timetable and budget.

All levels of people attended the meetings, including laboratory technicians, who had no patience with the conflict between Randy and Steve. They kept asking for orders as to what to do. They wanted to get busy on work, but didn't want their efforts wasted by a later reversal of decision. The statistician, Jack, saw the technicians' impatience and was starting to share it. The advisory board members were asking for so many different things to be done that Jack knew it was impossible to do them all. He started to assert himself at the meetings and kept reminding people about the time and money problems. The technicians were giving up on getting any advice from Randy and Steve. Jack then took a bold step. He started to talk to the technicians in private.

The technicians were straining at the leash to get going. Jack said that he thought they ought to get started with what they thought ought to be done because Jack agreed with them and he would defend their actions to Randy, Steve, and the advisory board. Jack braced himself, expecting to receive a lot of heat from Randy and Steve. Randy was delighted that somebody had made a decision, but the indecisive Steve couldn't say whether Jack's decision was good or bad. The advisory board was understanding and gradually became more approving of Jack's bold move, turning to him more and more to decide feasibility regarding time and money. Jack's advantage was that he was so conscious of the time and money problem. Steve understood the money problem but was a disaster regarding time. Randy was good at time but didn't have money judgment. Before too long, the advisory board was looking to Jack for general practical advice, and the technicians were happy to have their orders from the advisory board filtered through and interpreted by Jack. Steve and Randy wound up being treated politely by the advisory board, but had little influence. Jack's rise to power in the group did more than satisfy his ego. It got him entry into the design stage, where statisticians should be.

ON-THE-SPOT ANSWERS

There is pressure on a statistician in a group that doesn't exist so much in one-to-one consulting. It is the demand for on-the-spot answers in meetings. This runs against the grain of statisticians, who value slow, careful thought and considered answers.

Communicating Efficiently

The reason the on-the-spot answer is in such demand in a group is that it is so efficient to communicate with the group by speaking and so inefficient to send an understandable memorandum and expect them to read it. Also, it is difficult to hold meetings with busy people, and the group doesn't want to wait while you decide.

Consider the most common question a statistician is asked, "How big a sample size do I need?" Many times when I was in a research group meeting and having a hard time concentrating, someone would turn to me out of the blue and ask what I thought of the proposed sample size. Now every statistician knows that the sample size question is much easier to ask than to answer. The answer typically bogs down because the client has to make more decisions than he or she is capable of, such as deciding on power and meaningful alternative hypotheses. Still, groups decide things so quickly that if you don't give an answer right then and there, a decision will be made without you. They often can't or won't wait until the next meeting for the decision. The problem with thinking about it after the meeting and writing them a memo with your recommendations is not only one of their getting around to reading it, but one of discussing it by mail. The well-run meeting is extremely valuable and is a unique setting for decision making. Decision making by mail is nowhere near as efficient.

Thinking on Your Feet

It can be very difficult to think on your feet and give an answer to a group. Stage fright enters in, and you can answer only questions with which you are very familiar. I remember choking up on some very common questions. In one meeting, they turned to me to ask what sample size they would need to distinguish between two groups. They did their part in answering my questions, but I made some calculation errors and gave them a number that even they thought intuitively was wrong. I said I agreed and they waited patiently while I sweated out another calculation. I finally got it right, but was so embarrassed I apologized for the time it took. I still think they must wonder whether I am competent.

At another research team meeting with over ten people, we were deciding on an analysis of a huge data set. There were over five thousand observations on each of over fifty thousand sampling units, gathered over a period of more than ten years. One of the team members suggested, "Let's have the statistics people calculate the correlations so that we can each study them." My first thought was that there were way too many correlations for any individual to scan them visually, let alone agonize over each one. I knew I had to calculate the approximate number of them quickly to make the case against his suggestion. I wanted to get an agreement to eliminate most of the five thousand measurements on the grounds that they were so badly collected, with so much data missing, that they were useless to begin with. If his suggestion was not contradicted quickly, the several other team members who liked it would assume "the statistics people" would calculate them all and send printouts to the team members around the country. I knew it would work to send each one a copy of the printout in order to prove the absurdity of the suggestion by the sheer volume of material. (Note this clever ploy statisticians use: Give clients all the printout they ask for when it's ridiculously much.) That would be much work and expense, however, and I wanted to be less vengeful and more constructive. My plan was to talk them out of it fast before they moved on to another topic.

I had to come up with an argument that it was impossible for an individual to study all those numbers. My anxiety was high enough that I started to panic because I had a momentary mental block on counting. My head finally cleared enough to remember that there would be $n(n - 1)/2 \doteq (5,000)^2/2 = 12,500,000$. I have used that formula and taught it many, many times. The point is that pressure can have a devastating effect on one's ability to think. If you can't recall observing this in yourself during an oral exam, you can see it in athletic events in the final playoffs for the "world championship," when superb athletes make the most elementary mental errors. You can also see it in the word slips made by presidential candidates as the campaign goes to the wire.

I was actually worried that the 12.5 million was off by an order of magnitude. After checking its correctness with another statistician next to me, my next thought was to come up with an amount of time it would take to do 12.5 million such tasks and started to think of how many seconds there are in a year. I didn't have a pocket calculator; so I was desperately trying to multiply 60 by 60 by 24 on a scratch pad and found 86,400 seconds in a day. Trying to move faster and not have to multiply 86,400 by 365 exactly, I figured 86,400 was close enough to 100,000 and 365 was close enough to 400 to conclude that there are approximately $400 \times 100,000 = 4 \times 10^7 = 40,000,000$ seconds in a year. I then announced that working every day of the week for an eight-hour day for one year ought to do it, if one spent one second on each correlation. I got the result just in time. They were ready to move on to another topic, assuming I was going to mail each team member the 12.5 million correlations, just as I laid that figure of one year on them. It made the point perfectly and absolutely killed the suggestion. I then had the floor (hard to get at that meeting) and started arguing for eliminating most measurements due to their poor quality. That point won.

It was an important statistical victory. The moral of it is that my verbal argument, with figures to prove the impossibility of the task, was far better made right then and there. Timeliness was very important, and the pressure almost made me unable to do it. Groups full of experts who are very busy and difficult to assemble sometimes move fast with ripe opportunities for statistical points coming and going all the time.

Recently, I had a similar experience. I was working with a research team that was trying to get funding for future research and spent two days being grilled by thirteen visiting experts, including a sharp statistician. We were asking for a great deal of money, and the visiting experts were pushing us all hard. There was another statistician with me on the team. The team had been very resistant to our pressure to prepare better for the statistical working over I had anticipated, telling us not to worry so much.

The first day of the site visit went pretty well for our side, but the site visit chairman knew one of our researchers well and pulled him aside the first evening to say that we were in trouble because of sloppy statistical design. That investigator was really scared by the confidential warning and called me frantically that night to say we ought to do something fast about statistics or the team would lose several million dollars. He wanted to meet with the other statistician and me as well as two other investigators at 7:30 the next morning to draft a statistical statement for presentation to the site visitors at 8:30. That hour included typing time.

The statistical task to be accomplished in half an hour was horrendous. The three researchers were panicked, and they wanted us to make up for the fact that seventeen subprojects had been planned without statisticians being involved in choosing sample sizes. They were apologizing profusely that they hadn't listened to our warning them about the statistical weaknesses in the designs of the seventeen projects, but begged us to not quibble over the past.

The other statistician with me on the team, very technically competent, was inexperienced in team research. On the phone with me the evening before the day of our 7:30 A.M. meeting, he got his anger off his chest and agreed not to hit the researchers with a big "We told you so" at the morning meeting. He agreed to hold his temper and come across as helpful.

To add to the panic, my intestinal tract decided to act up, leaving me indisposed for twenty minutes of the 7:30–8:00 meeting. The researchers had more faith in my judgment than in my colleague's, simply because of his youth, but he was what they had for most of the meeting. The time I spent in the room with the five of us was very tense. The senior researcher wanted more of a coverup than my young colleague and I were willing to provide. I tried to control my temper but was as short with him as was reasonable. Everybody had to compromise if we were going to come up with a statement we could all live with. The final part of the drama was the fact that my young statistician colleague's salary depended on the project's success.

In spite of all the snapping at each other, we finally arrived at a statement. In it was included an example of a power calculation made by my colleague. I looked at it briefly, thought it was all right, and handed it to the typist at 8:05. We all went in to the big room on the second day of the examination at 8:30, planning to hand out the statistical statement to the site visitors as soon as it was typed. The secretary had done a nice typing job, had made a couple dozen photocopies, and handed me one to check over. I went over it quickly and said it looked fine.

One of our team was at the microphone and announced to the site visitors that a statement would be handed out now. I glanced down at the copy on my lap and something caught my eye. The example had a mistake on it. It was a wrong analysis for the design and the power was only .5. Then I started to clutch. I grabbed my colleague and showed it to him, not to scold him but to see if I was right. He agreed with me immediately. What to do? There was no time to retype anything, but we saw a way to white out a couple of lines and make corrections by hand. I then told the secretary, who is a very good one and a good sport to boot. She and my colleague ran off at top speed to make changes while I told our team member at the mike (loud enough for all to hear) that the typing wasn't done quite yet, but we'd have it in a few minutes. He gave me a look of exasperation, but recovered and went on speaking. When they were distributed in a few minutes, I sidled up to the statistician among the site visitors and said our calculations yielded only a power of about .5. I knew he would spot it. He understood and at coffee break I explained to him all that had happened.

It worked pretty well. The whole site visit team appreciated our hustle in trying to plug the statistical holes in the proposal. Later in the site visit, the statistician asked one of our investigators what he expected to get out of ten animals using a binomial response. The investigator was flustered and asked me to help him. I relied on the good old approximation that says middle fractions (.25 to .75) have two standard errors about $1 / \sqrt{n}$, about .30 in this case. Knowing that approximation, by the way, has been worth its weight in gold.

That site visit was rich with interaction. With over twenty people involved, thinking on one's feet was the order of the day. There was much probing by the site visitors, and we responded well the great majority of the time. I blew one question. It was directed at one of our team, who bounced it back to me. I wasn't listening and had to have it repeated. I saw that what had been written in the proposal by the on-the-spot team member was wrong. He had heard me say "multivariate discriminate analysis" at an earlier meeting and wrote it in his section. He hadn't told me about it, and I hadn't read it. The site visitors caught us in our failure to communicate. It wasn't a large embarrassment, but it didn't help. I admitted that it was not a correct analysis. The strategy was generally a success, though. The site review team wrote in their report that I was very well qualified for the job.

Being a statistician on a research team has given me some real headaches, but many more satisfactions. I also get better at it year by year and more enjoy the mixture of social life and work that research teams provide.

SUMMARY

• Some research teams drown in social friction and selfish personal agendas.

• Be patient with the social needs of team members.

• Don't convey the impression that the team's goals are unimportant. If you do, the team will exclude you from a position of influence.

• Show interest in the team's overall purpose, not just the statistical aspects.

• Get to know team members on a one-to-one-basis.

CHAPTER 11

Working On Your People Skills

Some statisticians are so naturally good with all people that by simply behaving instinctively they obtain good results. There are others, however, who get along well with only a few people. Whether a statistician wants to receive accurate feedback as to how he or she comes across and then go on to improve social skills is a major personal decision. Both of us have tried for several years to improve our dataside manner. We are satisfied enough with our progress to continue trying to improve it further. You may have no desire to spend energy analyzing or changing your style of consultation and may already function effectively as a consultant. In this chapter we offer four ways to think about the issue and some techniques for the adventurous reader.

FOUR LEVELS OF RESPONSE

Statisticians may respond to the people problems of statistical consultation at one of four levels.

The Conservative View

The first is the view that people who have emotional problems or hang-ups should not be allowed to do statistics or science. It is based on the belief that anyone who is so emotional that his or her personal needs get in the way of doing good science or statistics is simply too immature to be effective in these fields. This conservative view is held by quite a few statisticians who are very competent and highly respected in our field and can be defended on moral and ethical grounds, but it does ignore some political and economic realities.

Tolerating the Friction

The next, less extreme view of the people problems in statistics is that they are a headache, but nothing can be done about them. Statisticians with this philosophy agree that even scientists who have a lot of hang-ups and personal ego needs and are irritating to work with can do good science and are not to be ignored. In this view, nothing can be done about the statistician-client friction except to tolerate it. One outlet for statisticians who have to work with difficult clients is to get together and gripe about how stupid and uncooperative their clients are. Psychologists have named this outlet a game called "Ain't it awful?" People who play this game feel powerless to change the event, but get therapeutic benefit and sympathy from each other through complaining. It is also played frequently by other professional groups. For example, doctors gripe about their patients who won't take their advice. Lawyers complain that their clients lie to them.

Client-Consultant Matching

The third level of response is not as pessimistic as the first two, and it doesn't require that anyone change his or her personality. This approach, which we call client-consultant matching, is based on the belief that consultants work better with some clients than others and vice versa. We all have experienced personality clashes. There are many kinds of clashes. For example, two compulsive talkers can't get the other one to be a listener. They interrupt each other and are caught in a power play. This problem occurs when an insecure statistician and an insecure client try desperately to prove to each other how smart they are. In the matching model, the view is taken that neither the client nor the statistician can change. Obviously, the consultant best able to handle the client personally may not be the one most able technically.

Besides some relatively obvious personality conflicts that are to be avoided in matching consultant and client, there are some important attitudes on which consultants and clients should match. One of the most important matching variables is thoroughness. One of my colleagues is very thorough. She really hates to do quick-and-dirty jobs. She feels very unsatisfied with them and would like to be spared such consultation. She revels in the thorough, complete job. I, on the other hand, don't mind quick-and-dirty consultations. I comfortably rationalize that the clients who come to see me on a short-term basis either get what I can give them in a short time or they'll simply not get statistical advice. The basic difference between me and my colleague is that she is much more perfectionistic. She minds compromise a lot more than I do. When a client comes to me and apparently wants to do a very thorough job, I see if I can refer him or her to my thorough colleague. There are also clients who can't work with her because she takes too long and gives them too complicated an analysis. This thoroughness matching variable is psychologically very important. It is a matter of personal timing. You may have noticed that when you drive along a highway, you're uncomfortable with cars going too fast as well as with cars going too slowly. Clients can be just as upset with a statistician who is too perfectionistic as with one who is too hasty. Many clients don't plan their time well and are particularly bad at planning statistician time. They have no idea how long statistical things take.

The matching of client and consultant is an interesting problem in itself. It also can be quite threatening and frightening. It frequently conflicts with matching on expertise, in-which the client who has a multivariate problem is matched with a statistician in the group who knows the most about multivariate methods. I'm talking here about personality matching and style matching. One question is, "Who will do the matching?" It could be the boss of the group (that is, the most senior statistician), or it could be someone else selected for his or her great people wisdom. In this model, the matcher uses his or her own view of the consultants' person-alities, meets the clients on a screening basis, and then ar-rives at a statistician-client match on the basis of technical expertise as well as personality. If the consultants in the group all have respect for the matching person's judgment, this can work quite smoothly. The group may choose to be very discrete in talking about personality and avoid any pub-lic psychoanalysis of each other as to preferences for inter-personal relationships.

A problem with this matching model, if it is carried out very publicly, is that there may be one or more statisticians in the group very anxious to avoid the whole psychology business. They (like anyone else) don't want to be analyzed by other people, and certainly not by other statisticians, and may even be very uncomfortable with the whole topic of psychology in general. This attitude could stem from a per-sonal defensiveness or, just as likely, a sincere belief that all psychological knowledge is mere "junk" that shouldn't be used. The matching model, to the extent that it is psychologi-cal, could really disrupt a group of statisticians, forming two camps: those for and those against.

The main advantage of the matching model is that it is an attempt to do something about the people problem in sta-tistical consultation; yet it does not explicitly require some-one to change. Its shortcoming is that some people don't even like the awareness. In a special case, in which the entire group of statisticians is open and friendly and holds each other in warm regard, the group can be brought closer to-gether with the matching principle. By sharing of personal preferences in their interactions, the group will become more closely knit. If the group is able to open up to the extent that members feel open and comfortable about telling each other what each of them wants out of being a statistician, individual needs can be better met. Such open discussion may well bring out some frictions and hostilities in the group, but those differences have a chance of being resolved if the group members can handle them. Again, this approach is high risk for statisticians because of their high introversion rate, and judgment is required to see whether the Pandora's box should be opened. Some people become statisticians consciously or unconsciously to avoid people problems in general and would feel very cheated if forced to confront those issues in order to do statistical work. Consulting statisticians for industry, however, are screened partly for interpersonal skills and are expected to be somewhat good with people in order to do their jobs well.

Improving Interpersonal Skills

The fourth level of response involves a great deal of work on the part of the consultant wishing to undertake it. It is the commitment of an individual consulting statistician to improve his or her interpersonal skills. It is difficult, however, to work on improvement in interpersonal skills only in statistical consultation and not make any changes in the rest of one's life. The fact is that one has skill in interacting with other people, particularly in conflict resolution, either in all areas of life or in none of them. Everyone has more or less stress in all areas of life, statistical consultation being just one of them. The skills that are effective in reducing stress in a consultation are the same skills that reduce stress in interacting with one's spouse, parents, children, or clerks in a store. The development of these skills takes a great deal of work and a great deal of time and needs to be practiced in all settings. By a great deal of time, I mean something like two years.

Books and Courses.   The statistician who shows conspicuous defensiveness under a status insult will need a lot of training and practice to learn to mask that feeling from clients or to work through it. One advantage of the strategy of committing oneself to *personal* growth in interpersonal skills is that it does not so much threaten one's fellow consultants. The safest strategy for a consulting statistician who wants to learn more about human behavior with minimal personal risk is to read about it. There are all kinds of things written about human behavior, and one could take psychology courses or read psychology books. Anyone who is intelligent enough to be a consulting statistician already knows some psychology. Some people think they already know all they need to about human behavior, and what needs to be done is for the difficult people to shape up. Descriptions of human behavior are written up in many different fields from many points of view. Every religion has its own theory of what makes people tick and what, if anything, ought to be done about it. No one can function without some personal model of human behavior. The decision here is what to read and to whom to listen.

For the purposes of statistical consultation, very academic psychology books and courses are not useful. Psychoanalytic theory is interesting, but not helpful for the pragmatic consultant. Consulting statisticians who want to change their clients and themselves need more "savvy" than abstract psychological theory.

Getting Feedback.   The next stage in the plan for developing interpersonal skills involves getting feedback about how one appears and sounds to others. There is a technique that in one sense seems perfectly safe and, in another, totally frightening. It is the technique of being videotaped during personal interactions and studying the tape later with the sound both off and on. The safe thing about videotaping is if one does not like the results, one can erase the tapes, destroying that public record forever.

In recent years, while teaching a consultation course, I required that the students be videotaped during a fifteen-minute role play of consultation with an actor-client. This requirement scared some students out of their wits. Even though they understand that they can, if they do not like what they see, erase the tape, they are still very afraid of seeing it. Discussing their fear of making the videotape helps them see exactly what about it frightens them. I point out that if they are to role play a consultation with an actor-client and have a handful of students watch them (which they don't mind so much), showing the videotape to those same students is not showing them something new. To whom, then, is the videotape news? It is news to the person being videotaped.

The fact is, people will go to great length to avoid total self-awareness. Rapid advancement in improving one's interpersonal skills requires heavy doses of new self-awareness. The videotape machine will tell it like it is. A lot of people avoid being videotaped because they think the videotaping itself is so disruptive that reality will not be there for it to record. In my experience, and that of a colleague and many students, however, the videotape machine and taping personnel inflict a negligible amount of disruption on the process. In fact, reality is not disrupted and is well recorded.

Years ago I made several videotapes of my consultations, as did a colleague of mine. The consultations were absolutely real and all but one were at the first meeting with the client. I took these tapes to the annual statisticians' meeting and showed them to an audience of at least two hundred statisticians. The place was standing room only. My main goal was to make videotaping of statistical consultations a common practice, leading, I hoped, to a large library of tapes of real consultations. Although many statisticians were glad to see the tapes, they said openly that they would never make one themselves. The reason they expressed was not a fear of their seeing it themselves, but of having other statisticians see it and pick away at every little mistake at a technical level. Their fears are rational and well founded. Our field is perfectionistic, and statisticians tend to nitpick at each other for every little mistake.

(We have both done extensive work with audio and videotape equipment. I have not noticed much adverse reaction to the videotaping among my students. I work to set up safe environments in which the students first begin to use audiotaping equipment during their role play activities in class. I first videotape role plays and view them with the whole class. Students then move on to videotaping their sessions with actual clients. They initially are uneasy about the taping, but after a few weeks, most discomfort is gone.)

A very important aspect of the videotapes is their ability to provide feedback on nonverbal communication. This is done by watching your videotapes with the sound off. Communication experts say that the majority of the social impact of communication is nonverbal.

I have received feedback a number of times and had some sharp awakenings to things I do to turn people off as well as delight over my good points. Some of these reports are painful because I learned of characteristics I would like to change but cannot seem to. Generally, I tend to do well with people of high ego strength, but am not naturally reassuring and thus come across to shy people at times as insufferably arrogant and insensitive. If I'm facing a client who is ill at ease, frightened, and intimidated by statistics in general, I have to work very hard not to add to the person's fright. Adding to that fright decreases his or her ability to think clearly and his or her desire to cooperate with me. Although I tend naturally to be a thoughtless host, I go out of my way with such people to make them feel more comfortable.

I have also received considerable feedback on my consulting style. On two or three occasions, the information I received was both valuable and shocking. I had done role plays in which I thought I was using some of my most effective consulting communication tools. When the role plays were critiqued, the group was unanimous in regarding my communication style as offensive, arrogant, cold, and confrontive, almost exactly the opposite of what I had intended it to be. This feedback and the attendant review of the audio- and videotapes gave me much information about my consulting style and how to improve it.

On the other hand, I am unafraid of the arrogant, demanding client. I have a very sharp tongue and am capable of all kinds of cut-down tricks. I feel confident in a verbal street fight. I know another statistician, a much nicer person than I am, who just can't stand pushy clients who throw their weight around and are unappreciative of statistical help. That statistician gets so angry at such clients that he can't think effectively in their presence and spends some of his energy fantasizing vengeance.

Noting Nonverbal Cues.   Another technique for improving interpersonal skills is to pay attention to the feelings you have about people you see on the street: their walk, their facial expressions, the clothes they wear, and the cars they drive. These nonverbals give early clues about a number of things, such as their wealth and their degree of self-confidence. The impression formed on such evidence can be very wrong, but it is also difficult to avoid forming them. People judge each other, more than they would like to admit, by appearances. To illustrate, notice how hard politicians work to present their best visual side to the voters.

What picture does a client get upon entering your office? Does it look friendly or imposing? Does it look like somewhere an expert lives? Is it loaded with books with titles incomprehensible to the nonstatistician? There is a reason body language is so important. It's harder to lie with it. Think of the number of times you've heard a person say one thing by body language and something totally different in words. It takes a very good actor or actress to control all the nonverbal manifestations of what one is really feeling. Many muscles of the face, particularly the small muscles around the eyes, convey feeling. With videotaping, you can study the nonverbal messages you're sending.

One way to deepen your awareness of nonverbal dues is to watch a television drama with the sound turned off. Pay particular attention to the body language and notice your feelings toward the actors. Another method of obtaining feedback about one's impact on others is the feedback of honest, perceptive friends. (Actually, even some honest, perceptive *enemies* can do this well.) However, friends often try to spare your feelings and attempt to emphasize the good things. Enemies, of course, may have the opposite bias and want to punish you by holding a mirror up to your worst characteristics.

A PLACE FOR THE TIMID

Can the shy, introverted statistician be a good consultant? Yes. Definitely. Shy statisticians are typically unwilling and/or unable to present themselves as bold and confident as a technique to put a frightened client at ease, but they can still be very effective if they genuinely want to help their clients. Most clients will see beyond the shyness and find the genuine desire to help. However, the shy consultant who really does not want to help the client or is afraid to take responsibility for statistical decisions will be found out even more quickly than the insincere extrovert who has an exterior of confidence and reassurance. The helpful but shy consultant is only at high risk of losing frightened clients who need large, early doses of confidence and reassurance from statistical consultants.

Consultants should know what types of client behaviors elicit unproductive responses from them. They cannot do this fifteen minutes before a client arrives. Many of these introspective insights and their resolutions are lifelong activities. However, it is much easier to deal with people problems in a consulting session if consultants are aware of their effect on others and others' effects on them. The danger is that if a major anxiety has not been consciously recognized before the session, it may have a substantial impact on an unconscious level. Anxieties are best managed if they are acknowledged. Having an anxiety does not make you an inadequate statistician. Some anxieties are functional for a consulting statistician. It is necessary, for example, that statisticians feel confident that their calculations are correct. Other anxieties, such as embarrassment with eye contact, are dysfunctional because clients' facial reactions give valuable feedback.

We have both found tremendous satisfaction and reward in our statistical consulting with each new interpersonal skill we acquire. We expect to be much better at consulting five years from now and are enjoying the adventure. We hope you do, too. Let us hear about your experiences.

SUMMARY

- You may already have good people skills.

- Accurate, honest feedback regarding your people skills is invaluable. It can be obtained from friends and by viewing videotapes of yourself in interaction.

- Improving your people skills may take a long time, as much as two years.

- The most effective way to try to improve your interactions with clients is to try to improve them with everyone else, including store clerks, family, superiors, and subordinates.

- Shy statisticians can be very effective consultants.

CHAPTER 12

An Open Letter To Clients

This letter is addressed to the people who are necessary for us to be statistical consultants: our clients.* Serving them well is essential to our survival. We usually enjoy our contacts with them and the learning that ensues. We like to think we help them. We'd like to tell them what they can contribute to the statistical consulting session. There are attitudes they can hold and things they can do before and during the sessions to help their consultant succeed.

---

*Readers may find it helpful to send this letter, either as we've written it or modified to fit your needs, to your clients.

Dear Client,

Depending on the environment in which you work, you may or may not be able to choose your statistical consultant. In some situations where there is an ''in-house'' statistical consulting group, you may be a ''captive client'' who has no choice as to which consulting group or consultant to use. It may be that you apply to the consulting group for services and you are assigned a consultant. In other situations, you may have more choice as to who will be your statistical consultant.

If you can choose your consultant, there are some things you can do to get the best one for you. One strategy is to find other clients who have statistical needs similar to yours. Ask them where they get their statistical advice and how well it works. Alternatively, you may find people who are doing substantive work similar to yours and who know statisticians. Call them and ask for names of statisticians who are experienced in your general area of research. It is worthwhile knowing other users of statistical consultants in your company. Whom have they used and what has been their experience? This is also helpful for ''captive'' clients. If you know a statistician you trust, ask his or her opinion of your potential consultant. Different consultants have different areas of statistical expertise; so try to find one whose skills match your technical problems.

You will eventually identify a potential statistical consultant. Find out what experience this person has had in your area. It will be helpful to schedule a preliminary conversation to see whether the consultant's interests and abilities fit you and your problem. There are several issues to be discussed. Deming (1965) lists both consultant and client responsibilities. In deciding whether to retain a particular individual as your statistical consultant, you may ask to see an example of reports he or she has written on previous cases.

Something that makes it difficult for a client to find a good statistical consultant is the fact that statistics is still a very unstructured profession. People who keep records at sports events as well as people who have enough knowledge of higher mathematics to be awarded a Ph.D. in the field are both called statisticians. Statisticians are not licensed; they are not even certified. This means there is no formal method for the statistical community to deny one of its members privileges for technical incompetence or unethical behavior. The community of statisticians is loosely knit, with an extremely vague boundary as to who is and who isn't a statistician. There are people others see as statisticians because they act confident around numbers and have had a couple of statistics courses. Such people may be useful to you, but we consider a master's degree in statistics the minimum academic knowledge for a general-purpose statistician. A statistician who has less knowledge than that may be adequate for doing calculations, but not for making major decisions. Your expectations about the session and about statistical consultants in general play an important part.

You may have already done some analyses and be approaching the statistical consultant to check on its appropriateness. Your consultant hopes that you are open to the suggestion of other analyses that would add insights.

Or you may be approaching the consultant with a completed report in hand. Your consultant hopes that you are open to his or. her suggestions for improvement in statistical clarity.

Your statistician is thinking about three key questions as he or she works with you (Lurie, 1958, p. 57):

1. What are your ideas with respect to the *experiment* you are performing?
2. What are these ideas about with respect to the *scientific area* to which they refer?
3. How sure do you need to be of the correctness of these ideas? (More certainty requires more data; absolute certainty requires infinitely much data.)

Statisticians can do a better job if they have well-considered answers to these questions. A discussion of these questions will involve your describing the ideas you have about the experiment you are doing. Statisticians want you to describe the important factors, why you are interested in doing this study, what you hope to find out, and how this relates to the part of the world that you are interested in. They also want you to communicate how precise you wish to be in your inferences. This may be a statement as to how small you want your significance levels or probabilities of type II error to be. It may be an indication of the length of confidence intervals you desire.

You may be angry if your boss has ordered you to see a statistician. You may consequently want to prove that your boss is wrong in making you go to a statistical consultant and thus discount the consultant's suggestions. Your consultant hopes you can manage any resentment of being forced to see him or her. We think it is appropriate to discuss any such resentment you may have.

Your consultant wants to add to your expertise and what you have already done on your project, rather than to criticize your work. This is his or her orientation. If your consultant seems edgy and impatient, it is probably because he or she is trying too hard to achieve the best results. It is the consultant's job to assist you in doing good, effective research that is statistically sound.

Be realistic in your expectations of the statistical consultant. You have been working on your problem for months or years. The consultant has been consulting with you, as of the end of the first session, for one hour. He or she may need some time to learn the jargon and the key issues in your area. Most problems that involve statistical consultants are not solved statistically in one session. It may take a while to learn the language and the problems in order to come up with advice that will address your situation.

Be prepared to hear additional analyses or potential solutions from your consultant. Be open to redefining your goals in light of the statistical consultant's questions. His or her perspective as a statistician may open new directions for your research.

If the statistical consultant asks you seemingly endless questions, the intent is to assist you in doing good research, not to interrogate you or impugn your integrity. Although eagerness may make your consultant appear to lack tact, he or she merely wishes to collect all the relevant background information so as to be able to do a better job.

You may feel anxious before the first consulting session because you think you should know enough statistics to answer the question you are posing. Don't worry. Good consultants can work with clients who don't know any statistics. They just want you to know your own subject matter and cooperate with them. Consultants do like clients who want to learn statistics, however. There is so much to learn about statistics that your consultant is not worried that you will put him or her out of a job. Many clients learn how to do some basic statistical procedures in their area. They are then able to use consultants more effectively to handle more difficult problems.

Statistical consultants may wish to visit your laboratory. They mean not to check up on you, but to understand better how you and your laboratory technicians are doing your work. They may even have some suggestions that will help you in doing more statistically sound work on the basis of these visits.

Good statistical consultants have the goal of stimulating your statistical self-reliance. You may be encouraged to do more statistical thinking than you had initially planned to do. It may be much more effective in the long run for you to do some statistical work, rather than having your consultant do it all.

To prepare in advance for your consulting sessions, think about the statistical goals of this particular project and the questions you have.

There are some things that only you can do in the consulting session. For instance, statistical consultants cannot determine the basic goals of your research program or even its structure. They may be able to add on to the effectiveness of a structure that you have in place. Similarly, they may point out additional goals that could be achieved. They may also comment on whether your goals are statistically realistic with the resources you have at your disposal.

Before the consulting session, try to distinguish between your short- and long-range goals. Telling your consultant about this distinction may help him or her help you.

Another way you can prepare for the session is

to think about how much your statistical consultant needs to know about your field. Think about how you can present an overview of your area and then, more specifically, what problems your particular current project presents.

Consider what constraints there are to the solution of your problem. Collect information that may assist the consultant in understanding the issues in your field. If it is a legal case, what statutes or court decisions will be informative? What articles, reports, or memoranda will help the consultant develop some background information in your area?

Consider your goal for the entire consultation. What is your goal for the first session? Communicate your goals; make sure your consultant knows the time limits of your study. See the consultant early in your research. All consultants like the earliest possible involvement.

Think about the practical rewards for you and your statistical consultant. What fees are you paying? How are you handling issues relating to memoranda, publication, authorship, and publication credit? The importance attributed to publication varies widely across working environments. In some companies it is vital to your advancement; in others the only thing that counts is making a contribution to successful projects.

What use will be made of the statistical consultant's reports? Will you need his or her permission to use it or to quote from it in subsequent publications? Will the statistical consultant be able to use your data in subsequent articles or publications?

What type of support do you want from your statistical consultant? This is a key question affecting the type of relationship you will have.

How much statistics do you want to be responsible for learning or for doing? Communicate these goals.

Time and money estimates are difficult to make at the beginning of a study. Nonetheless, they are vital. Help your consultant make at least a rough estimate. One effective strategy is to consider the best and worst cases and see if the project's cost can be estimated in these two extreme situations.

One of the key ingredients that determines whether or not a statistical consultation will ''work'' is whether or not you and your organization are ready to receive the statistical advice given. Are you in a position to be able to take this advice? Are there vested interests in your organization that are opposed to your research? Recognizing at the outset that a problem is unsolvable because there are powerful people who want it to remain unsolved can save your time and the consultant's.

Your consultant may not know all the statistical answers to the questions you ask. He or she may have to discuss your problem with computer experts and other statisticians. Similarly, your consultant's work may involve various support personnel, such as computer programmers. Is this all right with you? What aspects of your problem are confidential? Will this confidentiality be a problem if the consultant feels the need to discuss your situation with other consultants? That your consultant refers to other statisticians may look, on the surface, like a sign of weakness or incompetence. It also indicates a willingness to recognize his or her limitations. It suggests a willingness to be realistic about what he or she knows and doesn't know and to seek additional support.

Some consultants like you to send a brief summary of your problem to them before the first session. In it, describe the area in which you are doing the research and the particular purpose of your project. Describe the type of data you have gathered or propose to gather, indicating what people or things you will measure, what variables you will measure at what times, and any major difficulties associated with gathering this data. Specify the purpose of the overall research program and your purpose in employing the statistical consultant. What questions would you like to get answered? What issues would you like to get resolved? Indicate your time and money limits and describe the resources available to you.

Frequently seek clarification during your consultation sessions. Ask for help in understanding the concepts, suggestions, and ideas being presented. Less is accomplished if you do not understand the consultant's ideas, their implications for the project, and how you will act on them. Similarly, ask for feedback from the consultant to see whether your communication has been understood. Some statisticians hesitate to ask questions about technical details they think they should have already understood. You can make your consultant more effective by asking whether or not he or she has understood certain key points and by asking for a paraphrase of them. You can then see whether you both understand.

It is important that you tell your consultant about any sticky problem in the study. This is tough to do but essential if the statistical work is to be relevant and accurate. It is better to have study problems aired in your early sessions. It is less painful to deal with difficulties with this person than to have them discovered later by a referee or critic in your discipline. Your consultant is used to hearing serious problems. These problems can also show up in subsequent research, when it is impossible to replicate your results.

Will your consultant provide you with a written

copy of his or her input to the project? When? In what form? What questions will be addressed in the document? There is value in written communication of key points between the parties in a statistical consultation. They can often be communicated more clearly, and with less danger of loss, by writing them down. Though this seems to be time-consuming, it is our experience that the payoff in terms of money saved and misinterpretation avoided can far offset the cost of writing the memo in the first place.

You may want to use audiotapes to record the statistical consulting sessions so that you can review them. The recordings may allow you to relax more during the session by reducing your worry about catching every word the consultant says. However, you should not rely on the recording to clarify the session. Your best chance to clarify critical points is to ask the consultant when the point arises what was meant. During the session, your consultant may lapse into silence for extended periods of time. There is not necessarily something wrong. It is likely that your statistical questions require your consultant to think hard and he or she needs to focus attention. Sometimes during the first session it is to your mutual advantage to negotiate your working relationship. You both want to understand who will have what responsibility.

Experience in finding and using statistical consultants is very valuable. Take the assertive approach and you'll soon be good at it. Both you and your consultants are very human and trying your best. If neither of you loses sight of that, you'll be all right.

REFERENCES

Boen, J. "The teaching of interpersonal relationships in statistical consulting," *The American Statistician, 26,* 30–31, 1972.

Boen, J., and Fryd, D. "Six-state transactional analysis in statistical consulting," *The American Statistician, 32,* 58–60, 1978.

Boen, J., and Smith, H. "Should statisticians be certified?" *The American Statistician, 29,* 113–114, 1975.

Bross, I. D. J. "The role of the statistician: Scientist or shoe clerk," *The American Statistician, 28,* 126–127, 1974.

Cameron, J. M. "The statistical consultant in a scientific laboratory," *Technometrics, 11, 247–254, 1959.*

Daniel, C. "Some general remarks on consulting in statistics," *Technometrics, 11,* 241–245, 1969.

Deming, W. E. "Principles of professional statistical practice," *The Annals of Mathematical Statistics, 36,* 1883–1900, 1965.

Feinstein, A. R. "Clinical biostatistics VI. Statistical 'malpractice'—and the responsibility of a consultant," *Clinical Pharmacology and Therapeutics, 11,* 898–914, 1970.

Hunter, W. G. "The practice of statistics: The real world is an idea whose time has come," *The American Statistician, 35,* 72–76, 1981.

Hyams, L. "The practical psychology of biostatistical consultation," *Biometrics, 27,* 201–211, 1971.

Joiner, B. J. "Consultant's interview—style checklist," unpublished class notes, 1980.

Lurie, W. "The impertinent questioner: The scientist's guide to the statistician's mind," *American Scientist, 46,* 57–61, 1958.

Marquardt, D. W. "Statistical consulting in industry," *The American Statistician, 33,* 102–107, 1979.

Marquardt, D. W. "Criteria for the evaluation of statistical consulting in industry," *The American Statistician, 35,* 1981.

Miller, R. G., Jr., Efron, B., Brown, B. W., Jr., and Moses, L. E. *Biostatistics Casebook*, New York: Wiley, 1980.

Salsburg, D. S. "Sufficiency and the waste of information," *The American Statistician, 27,* 152–154, 1973.

Snee, R. D., Boardman, P. J., Hahn, G. J., Hill, W. J., Hocking, R. R., Hunter, W. G., Lawton, W. H., Ott, R. L., and Strawderman, W. E. et al. "Preparing statisticians for careers in industry: Report of the ASA Section on Statistical Education Committee on Training Statisticians for Industry," *The American Statistician, 34,* 65–80, 1980.

Turner, A. Unpublished class notes, *Harvard Business School*, 1979.

Woodward, W. A., and Schucany, W. R. "Bibliography for statistical consulting," *Biometrics, 33,* 564–565, 1977.

Zahn, D. A., and Isenberg, D. J. "Non-statistical aspects of statistical consulting," *1979 Proceedings of the Section on Statistical Education of the American Statistical Association,* 67–72.